D0396718

The Duke Ellington Primer

By Dempsey J. Travis

Other Urban Research Press Best Sellers By Dempsey J. Travis

Don't Stop Me Now
An Autobiography of Black Chicago
An Autobiography of Black Jazz
An Autobiography of Black Politics
Harold: The People's Mayor
Real Estate Is The Gold In Your Future
Racism: American Style A Corporate Gift
I Refuse To Learn To Fail
Views From The Back Of The Bus During WWII And Beyond

November 1953, left to right, Harold Washington, who became Mayor of Chicago in 1983, Marcella Davis, Duke Ellington, Moselynne Travis, and Dempsey J. Travis, author

The Duke Ellington Primer

Urban Research Press, Inc.

Copyright© 1996 Urban Research Press, Inc.
840 East 87th Street, Chicago, Illinois 60619, U.S.A.
Printed in the United States of America
First Edition
ISBN: 0-941484-25-4

Library of Congress Cataloging-in-Publication Data

Photo Credits:
Smithsonian: 1, 2, 3, 9, 12, 15, 35, 39, 40
Johnson Publishing Co.: 103, 127
Theater Historical Society of America: 43, 88, 89
All other pictures are the property of Urban Research Press, Inc.

ACKNOWLEDGMENTS

For almost 70 years I have been a Duke Ellington addict. I was initially introduced to the magic of his music via a radio broadcast in 1928 from the Cotton Club in New York City. Radio waves sustained my interest in his music until I finally heard him in person in 1931 at the Oriental Theater in Chicago.

Duke's musical excellence inspired me. Ellington's genius made his most intricate compositions seem effortless. Year after year he turned out musical home runs. "Black and Tan Fantasy," 1927; "Black Beauty," 1928; "The Mooch," 1929; "Ring Dem Bells," 1930; "Mood Indigo," 1931; "It Don't Mean a Thing If It Ain't Got That Swing," 1932; "Sophisticated Lady," 1933; "Drop Me Off in Harlem," 1934; "In a Sentimental Mood," 1935 and each year thereafter until his year of transition in 1974.

The Ellington contributions are alive and well and being played throughout the world. Members of my literary ensemble who contributed to making the Duke Ellington Primer happen were my wife, Moselynne E. Travis; Ruby B. Davis, senior researcher; Richard Bjorklund, senior editor, and Amanda Adams, junior editor and administrative assistant.

Other persons who have been helpful are Geraldine de Haas and Josie Childs of Jazz Unites; Archie Motley of the Chicago Historical Society, as well as Dorothy Lyles, librarian; Robert Miller, curator; Mary A. Williams, assistant curator, and Michael Flug, archivist, all of the Vivian G. Harsh Collection of Afro-American History at the Carter G. Woodson Regional Library in Chicago.

This book is dedicated

to Wynton Marsalis

The

Jazz Torchbearer

HONOR DENIED

In 1965 when he was 66 years old, the Pulitzer Prize Music Committee recommended Duke Ellington for a special award. That recommendation was turned down by the full Pulitzer committee and America's most creative composer said:

> Fate is being very kind to me.Fate doesn't want
> me to be too famous too young.

Duke Ellington
1965

HONORS RECEIVED
(7 of 226)

The President's Medal
    Award for special Merit-presented by the Art Director's   1958
    Club

The Spingarn Medal
    Achievement Award-presented by the National Association   1959
    for the Advancement of Colored People

Gold Medal
    "Musician of the Year"-presented by the Mayor of the City   1965
    of New York

Gold Medal
    Presented by the City if Chicago, Illinois   1965

Medal
    Special cast with bust of Ellington-presented by the City of   1965
    Paris, France

President's Choice Medal
    Presented in the name of President Lyndon B. Johnson   1966
    by the American Ambassador, Madrid, Spain

Presidential Medal of Freedom
    The highest civilian award of the United States-presented   1969
    by President Richard M. Nixon

Contents

Contents

PROLOGUE

Few nonfiction writers have ever been able to capture the composite picture of one person's life within the covers of a single book, especially when that individual was mercurial and noncategorical as Duke Ellington, whose creative power produced more than 2,000 songs in 58 years.

Every one of Duke Ellington's songs is a story unto itself. Some of his compositions are about lost love, others are about new love and still others about old and unforgettable love. His 1945 song "I Am Just a Lucky So And So" is about the loss of an unfaithful lover.

The moods of Ellington's songs are limitless. He may submerge 10 feet deep in the ballet water music of "The River" (1970) and then with the stroke of a single chord he may emerge riding a camel across the Sahara Desert in a "Caravan" (1937).

No facet of life escaped Duke Ellington's musical attention. Even railroad trains could not elude his creativity. Duke saw trains as both good and evil. Evil in that he found their Jim-Crow seating inhumane. Yet his ears would not permit him to hear the "you boys" comments of racist conductors. His mind tuned out the drawl of racism while he creatively listened to the sounds of the train. He musically seized the clickety clack of the train wheels, the lonesome and mourning sounds of a train whistle in the middle of the night, and the hissing noise of a steam driven locomotive engine as it pulled into a station. The train sounds that he heard enabled him to write "Choo Choo (I Gotta Hurry Home)" (1924), "Daybreak Express" (1934), "Happy Go Lucky Local" (1947) and "Night Train to Memphis" (1968). Duke's train music gave his listeners the benefit of a train ride without their ever having to board a train.

Although I boarded the Ellington train 65 years ago, I am certain that my personal observations are only a snapshot of the great man's life onstage, backstage and in the streets. Therefore I enlisted the assistance of more than 100 musicians who boarded the train many stops ahead of me. Collectively, I believe we have covered the highlights of Duke and his times.

To attempt to reconstruct Ellington's life and times with fewer guides would be to reenact the fable about the blind men and the elephant: The man who touched the elephant trunk said, "It is a big nose." Another holding his tail retorted, "It is a long tail." Yet another declared with absolute authority, "It is a big foot." Duke Ellington was by no means such a dismembered man.

What I have attempted to present in this "primer" is a hands on work that might aid us in understanding Duke Ellington's contribution to civilization.

Dempsey J. Travis

1996

Edward Kennedy Ellington at the age of 5.

1 ~ SPIRITUALLY HE WAS ALWAYS THE DUKE

On April 29, 1899, in a middle class home located in the Negro section of northwest Washington, D.C. at 2129 Ward Place, Daisy Kennedy Ellington gave birth to a baby who was delivered by a midwife named Eliza Jane Johnson. The baby boy was given the Christian name Edward, the second name of his father, James Edward Ellington. His middle name would be Kennedy, in honor of his maternal grandparents, James William Kennedy and Alice Kennedy, who owned the house in which he was born.

His grandfather, James William Kennedy, was a District of Columbia police captain.

His grandmother, Alice Kennedy, was a housewife who was occupied taking care of their ten children.

Edward Kennedy Ellington's mother treated her baby like a

prized jewel. She did not want his little toes to touch the floor. Her sparkling and penetrating brown eyes and long, thin, queenly fingers were never more than a few feet from her copper-colored prince until he reached the age of four.

Daisy Ellington was overly protective of her child because her first pregnancy ended in miscarriage. During her second pregnancy, she took a ride on a ferryboat that sank. This harrowing experience was often retold to Edward Kennedy Ellington during his adolescent years, making him a very fearful, superstitious adult.

Fear kept him from riding in a plane unless it was absolutely necessary. Some 31 years after his birth, he superstitiously thought Friday the 13th was his

Daisy Kennedy Ellington was a charming and loving mother to young Edward.

good luck day because of a very successful opening for his orchestra on that date at Chicago's Oriental Theater.

On Edward's first day of liberation, in the summer of 1903, Mrs. Ellington's precious child wandered onto the front yard of his grandmother's house and stumbled over a lawn mower bruising the fourth finger of his left hand. The scratch on his pinkie was treated as a major emergency by Daisy Ellington, who called the entire family into conference to decide what to do about a mishap that could ordinarily be healed by a mother's kiss.

The strength of his mother's obsessive devotion must have permeated Young Edward's psyche with the notion that he was something special. She constantly instilled in him the values that gave him great self esteem by reciting that he was a blessed child who could accomplish anything in the world that he wanted.

In the fall of 1903, little Edward was stricken with pneumonia. Mrs. Ellington frantically called two of the best colored doctors in the District of Columbia to come and work the miracle of healing on her precious baby. After the doctors performed their miracle and assured Mrs. Ellington that little Edward would survive, she maintained a 24-hour vigil at his bedside until his elevated body temperature dropped to normal. A series of Edward's hot sweats caused her to change his bedding several times during the course of the night.

Duke Ellington recites his bout with this respiratory ailment in his biography "Music Is My Mistress," written 69 years after the event. "I could not speak, but I can still see my mother, kneeling, sitting, standing to lean over my bed praying and crying, and repeatedly wailing, 'My own child does not even recognize me,'" Ellington recalled.

When little Edward Ellington was 5 years old, his mother raised his age to 6 so he could skip kindergarten and enter grammar school at the first grade level. She dressed her little darling like a young prince and sent him off to Garnet Public School, just a couple of blocks away. Every morning, rain or shine, she secretly followed him right up to the school playground and watched as he disappeared behind the schoolhouse door. Daisy Ellington never suspected that her son was very much aware of her Sherlockian sleuthing. At 3:15 p.m. every day she could be found waiting at the front door of the school or nervously standing on the sidewalk in front of their house awaiting his arrival.

The Washington Senators' Griffith Park is where Ellington peddled peanuts, popcorn and chewing gum.

Ellington started taking private piano lessons when he was 7 years old from music teacher Marietta Clinkscales (her real name). Mrs. Clinkscales came to the house twice a week to give him instructions and rap lightly on his knuckles when he made a mistake. Nevertheless, Edward's interest in baseball and art over-

James Ellington was employed at 1467 Rhodes Island Avenue as a butler.

shadowed his interest in music. His artistic talents must be credited to the Kennedy side of the family because several of his uncles produced work of exhibit quality. Edward Kennedy Ellington dreamed of someday being a great artist like them.

He was so in love with baseball that he got a job after school hawking peanuts, popcorn, candy and chewing gum at the Washington Senators' Griffith Park, at North Capital and Massachusetts Avenues. Gradually he began to skip more music lessons than he attended. But his love affair with baseball waned just like his interest in music, and he soon lost interest in the sport.

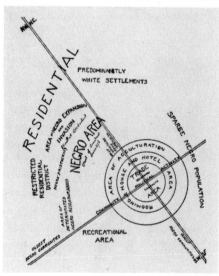

The General Ecological Organization of the City of Washington in the early Nineteen hundreds.

James Edward Ellington, the Duke's dad, never completed elementary school but carried himself with the demeanor of a Harvard graduate as he performed his daily tasks as a butler. His handsome good looks

President Woodrow Wilson

complemented his elegant manner. Moreover, James Edward had excellent language skills, which served him well as an employee of Dr. Middleton F. Cuthbert, a prominent white physician who lived in the big house at 1467 Rhode Island Avenue. Mr. Ellington's household authority was limited to supervising the cook and the maid as well as graciously opening and closing the front door for members of the family and their guests. He comported himself like the chief executive officer of a major business and talked like a man who had plenty of money. Mr. Ellington treated his wife Daisy and son Edward as though he was a millionaire, though he resided in his mother-in-law's home.

In 1917, during World War I, he quit his house steward position and rented a big single-family house on "K" Street, in the upscale, ethnically changing northwest area. He augmented his income by renting out rooms in the mansion-size dwelling to wartime workers. In addition, he catered big parties and occasionally served as a part-time waiter in the White House of President Woodrow Wilson until he got a full-time job working in the blueprint department of Washington's Navy Yard.

Little Edward Ellington was greatly influenced by the way his father dressed and talked. And his good manners were also affected by his mother Daisy, a graduate of the "M" Street High School, predecessor to the classic Dunbar Public High School, one of only two secondary schools for colored children in the District of Columbia.

Ellington worshiped his mother and admired his father, who agreed that he should pursue his dream and become an artist. Hence, piano lessons were allowed to fade faster than sundown in December.

The summer before graduating from grammar school, young Ellington visited his mother's brother, John Kennedy, an accomplished artist who lived on Catherine Street in Philadelphia. During this visit in the "City of Brotherly Love" he heard a piano player a year older than himself whip the piano keys until they figuratively "smoked." That young musician's name was Harvey O. Brooks, who had a tremendous left-hand keyboard swing like

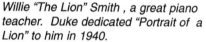

Willie "The Lion" Smith , a great piano teacher. Duke dedicated "Portrait of a Lion" to him in 1940.

Eubie Blake, top notch piano player and composer of "Memories of You" and "I Am Wild About Harry."

Eubie Blake and Willie "The Lion" Smith. Brooks, a heralded pianist-composer, died in Los Angeles, California, in June, 1968, at the age of 70.

When Edward returned to Washington, he was stricken with a severe case of the flu that was threatening to turn into pneumonia, confining him to the house for two weeks. During Ellington's convalescence, the piano performance of young Brooks continued to bubble and boil in Ellington's consciousness to the point that it rekindled his interest in the piano. Tinkering around on the piano, Ellington fashioned his first musical composition "Soda Fountain Rag." The title arose from weekends Ellington spent working as a soda jerk at the Poodle Dog Cafe on Georgia Avenue. "Soda Fountain Rag," though it was never recorded or copyrighted, was played by Ellington around Garnet School whenever the opportunity presented itself. His playing drew much attention from the blossoming young girls. During this period Ellington also attracted the attention of young men who wanted to share some of the spotlight he was getting from the tender female flowers.

Edgar McEntree, the first member of Ellington's entourage, was a fine looking young boy from a wealthy Negro family. His folks dressed Edgar as if they were members of Washington's "Blue Bloods." One afternoon Edgar told Edward that if he wanted to be his constant companion he would need to have a title. Thus, he anointed Edward Kennedy Ellington "Duke," a nickname befitting the son of James and Daisy Ellington and one that he wore with distinction into eternity.

Young Edgar McEntree became a party crasher and a hawker for Duke Ellington, the piano player. As an advance man, Edgar milled around among party goers and bragged about how well Ellington could play the piano. When Duke made his grand entrance he was a sought-after commodity who never objected to playing the piano. Ellington typified a sheltered mama's boy eager to display his newly discovered talent.

Duke repeatedly played his second composition, "What You Gonna Do When The Bed Breaks Down?" that was a big hit with the rubbing and hugging, slow-drag dancing bunch. Luckily for Duke the kids liked his song and requested it over and over again. Duke had only one other song in his musical repertory, his "Soda Fountain Rag." He could play his two compositions in a number of dance tempo variations from 2/4 time (Charleston), to 3/4 (waltz), and 4/4 (fox trot). This technique he employed with many of his compositions throughout the balance of his long career. He would also change titles to old songs. "Never No Lament" and "Concerto for Cootie" later became very popular songs under new names: "Don't Get Around Much Anymore" and "Do Nothing 'Till You Hear From Me." The Duke's classic "Mood Indigo" was once known as the "Dreamy Blues."

On the party circuit, Duke discovered that there was always a pretty girl standing at the side of the piano whenever he played. He was so delighted with the admiration he was getting from the ladies that he buried notions of ever becoming a professional athlete or artist.

In 1913, the 14-year-old Duke skipped his eighth grade classes to go to the Gayety Burlesque Theater. There he observed gorgeous show girls who looked good in the clothes they wore and looked even better as they tantalizingly stripped their garments off piece by piece.

At the same age, the Duke started hanging out at Frank Holliday's Pool Room on "T" Street between Sixth and Seventh, next door to the Howard Theater. Frank's place was not an ordinary neighborhood pool room, but a top-of-the-line billiard parlor where high school and college kids from all over Washington gath-

8

The Gayety Burlesque Theater is where young Ellington fulfilled some of his youthful fantasies.

ered to watch great pool sharks. Players crawled out of corner pockets of every pool den in the District to shoot pool at Frank Holliday's.

Duke, fascinated by the pool hustlers and their hip behavior, also enjoyed listening to the conversations among the Pullman porters and dining-car waiters who also hung out at Holliday's. They were always "fish bone" clean from the top of their heads to the soles of their shoes. Dressed as sharply as dancers preparing to perform in the main event, these fellows had a lot to say about their travels and women in far-flung cities. Duke's toes tingled with excitement when he would overhear them say, "I was in Chicago last night," or "I am going out to San Francisco tomorrow." Unlike the Duke's own father, these men had been to some big towns and heard some big talk. Duke wanted to emulate the railroad men because in the colored community they represented both "cool" and respectability.

Not generally known outside of the Negro community was that Pullman porters and waiters were often college graduates stuck in service jobs which were considered the best a racist job market would offer men of color.

James P. Johnson, piano player and composer of "If I
Could Be With You Tonight", "Charleston", and
"Carolina Shout". He also accompanied Bessie Smith
and Ethel Waters in the 1920's.

2 - GIGGING WITH THE DUKE

Oﾠne of Duke's first professional gigs as a teenage musician was traveling with a man named Joe, whose last name Ellington could never recall. Joe's act was half magic and half fortune telling. The young piano player, of course, did not have a clue about what he was supposed to do until Joe instructed him to ad lib on the piano and blend the music to the character of Joe's performance. Duke was very pleased to discover his ability to musically capture the mood of the act in the same fashion that pit pianists captured the diverse emotions of movie stars and scenes in popular silent movies.

Ellington also got gigs playing relief piano for the orchestras of Doc Perry, Louis Brown, Lester Dishman and others. It was then that Duke started alternately throwing his left and right hand in the air about six inches above the keyboard while accompanying a

The sophisticated Oliver "Doc" Perry, was Duke's piano parent.

singer or instrumentalist. He adopted this flashy style of playing after observing "Lucky" Roberts, a featured pianist at the Howard, the premier colored vaudeville theater in Washington, D.C. Charles Luckyeth Roberts died at the age of 71 on February 5,1968, in New York City after a long career as a pianist and composer.

Although Duke then knew how to play only about four songs-excluding his own two compositions-he was considered a good pianist because he had effectively adopted the keyboard style of "Lucky" Roberts. He continued using that style throughout his career as his flair, good looks and sophisticated demeanor made

The Howard Theater, in the District of Columbia

Charles "Lucky" Roberts, a talented pianist with large hands that could spread twelve keys.

him an excellent candidate for gigs at society dances and parties.

After he had been playing with the Louis Thomas Orchestra for a couple of years, Ellington was sent on a solo gig at the Ashland Country Club, where he was to play dinner music for a room full of millionaires. As Ellington was walking out of the door of Thomas's office enroute to the gig, Mr. Thomas said, "Play atmosphere and conversation music and collect $100 and bring me $90." Duke delivered the $90 to Thomas that night. But the very next morning he went straight to the telephone-book office and placed a classified display ad that read "Irresistible 'Jass' furnished for our select patrons..." Duke reasoned that since a large number of people in Washington were out-of-town war workers, they would not know the difference between Meyer Davis, Louis Thomas and Duke Ellington.

Telephone-book advertising was very effective and Ellington

began sending out four or five bands a night under his own banner. Business was so good that he bought a new Chandler car and a house at 2728 Sherman Avenue in June, 1919, for his new wife Edna and his son Mercer, born March 11, 1919.

The youthful Duke Ellington on a gig at Louis Thomas' Cabaret in 1919. Left to right: Sonny Greer, Bertha Ricks, Ellington, Mrs. Conaway and Sterling Conaway.

The 1919 Irresistible 'Jass' telephone book ad that put Duke on the music map in Washington, D.C.

In June, 1918, Duke had "jazzed" Edna Thompson, a neighbor's beautiful 17-year-old virgin daughter, and was pushed by both sets of parents into a shotgun marriage several months before their baby was born. According to Mercer, Duke never wanted a son but rather a daughter.

Duke had dropped out of Armstrong Manual Training School in February, 1917, three months before he was to graduate. Prior to leaving school he won an NAACP art scholarship to Pratt Institute in Brooklyn, New York. Dropping out of school was prompted by the money he anticipated making in wartime by working for the United States Navy as a messenger, painting signs and backdrops for the Howard Theater, designing placards for social functions, and playing the piano.

14

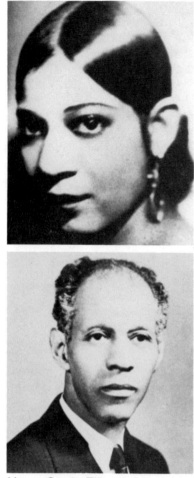

A picture of Edna Thompson Ellington, Duke's wife, taken in the early 1930's.

Henry Grant, Ellington's neighbor and harmony teacher.

The young piano player's propaganda claims exceeded his ability as a jazz musician to produce or perform anything of real substance on the keyboard. To protect his reputation required some serious study, a habit he had not yet acquired. He got a fellow piano player, Doc Perry, to teach him how to read music. Henry Grant, a neighbor and Dunbar High School music teacher, agreed to show him the ground rules of Harmony 101. A broader understanding of the basic elements of music later enabled Duke to employ his own creative chord structures.

Ellington continued to broaden his musical landscape by listening to great piano players like James P. Johnson, Willie "The Lion" Smith and others. Percy "Brushes" Johnson, a drummer friend of Duke's, had a player-piano in his house and a piano roll by the legendary James P. Johnson, unrelated to "Brushes" Johnson. Duke went to Percy's home and listened to the music produced on the perforated paper piano roll. By mechanically slowing the tempo of the music roll, Duke could study the piano keys as they were activated. Duke listened intently to sounds emanating from the piano and eagerly watched the keys as the roll played Johnson's very popular "Carolina Shout." After some weeks of listening and practicing Ellington finally got the number down pat.

When pianist James P. Johnson came to the District of Columbia to play at Convention Hall, Duke's fans insisted that he get up on the bandstand and cut (beat) him playing his own song. Johnson, master musician that he was, went along with the act and let young Ellington do his number. Johnson joined Duke's young fans in applauding him long, loudly and enthusiastically. For the rest of the night, Duke leaned over the piano keyboard digesting every note and chord change that Johnson played. Ellington said that what he learned that evening was equivalent to a semester at a conservatory of music.

After the dance, James P. Johnson selected Duke to be his personal guide on a tour of Washington night spots. A respectful relationship between the two men jelled and their friendship became a very important bridge for Ellington when he, several years later, went to play in New York City.

Fred Guy and Duke Ellington, two roaring twenties dudes in New York City in 1925. Guy worked with the Ellington band from 1925 to 1949.

3 - DROP ME OFF IN HARLEM

Duke, like his fellow musicians across the face of urban America, both colored and white, felt that they were not in the big time unless they had been musically tested in New York City. All were in awe of the honor roll of great entertainers and musicians working in the "Big Apple" during the Harlem Renaissance period,1920-1930. Both Harlem and midtown Manhattan were crowded with such legendary talents as Fletcher

Fletcher Henderson, the orchestra leader at the Roseland Ballroom just off Broadway in midtown Manhattan.

Bert Williams set the pace for all comedians, black and white, during the first 25 years of the 20th century.

Henderson, Paul Whiteman, Florenz Ziegfeld, George Gershwin, Vincent Lopez, Eubie Blake, Eddie Cantor, Al Jolson, Bert Williams, Noble Sissle, Florence Mills, Sophie Tucker, Edith Wilson, Ethel Waters, W.C. Handy, Mamie Smith, Bessie Smith,

Ethel Waters, a theater singing and recording star in the 1920's. She later became a Broadway actress and movie star.

Bill Robinson, the legendary tap dancing star in the movies and on Broadway. He, like Duke, was beyond categorizing.

Early 1924, Sonny Greer, Charles Irvis, "Bubber" Miley (seated), Elmer Snowden, Otto Hardwick and Ellington at the Hollywood Cafe.

Clara Smith, Irene and Vernon Castle, Miller and Lyles, Bill "Bojangles" Robinson, Alberta Hunter and Fess Williams, among others.

On March 5,1923, Wilbur Sweatman hired Duke with Otto Hardwick, Arthur Whetsol and Sonny Greer for a one-week gig at the Lafayette Theater in New York City's Harlem. They returned to Washington immediately following the Harlem gig and subsequently made a second trip to the "Big Apple" in June of the same year with a five-piece band. Hired to accompany Clarence Robinson, the talented and popular choreographer, the band was stranded when the gig did not materialize.

Duke and the boys, suddenly jobless, stayed together through the summer, hustling gigs at Barron Wilkins' Cafe in Harlem, the Music Box in Atlantic City and occasionally the Winter Garden Building in New York City's Times Square. The band soon became known in New York music circles as the Washingtonians. Personnel consisted of what later became the core of the legendary Duke Ellington Orchestra: the initial leader was Elmer Snowden, a banjo player; the sidemen were Arthur Whetsol, trumpet; Otto Hardwick, saxophone; Sonny Greer, drums; and Duke Ellington, piano.

The Washingtonians' first sustaining gig in New York City began September 1,1923, in a basement cabaret called the Hollywood Cafe, a speakeasy located on 49th Street between Broadway and Seventh Avenue in midtown Manhattan. The cafe could accommodate only 130 patrons and the band's five musicians were cramped into a small space. At the time, Duke and his wife Edna lived uptown in Harlem at a rooming house run by Leonard Harper, a very fair-skinned Negro with silky straight hair. Harper,who could have passed for white, was a top-flight choreographer and producer at Connie's Inn, a "for whites only" cafe in colored Harlem next door to the Lafayette Theater on Seventh Avenue, and the Kentucky Club, also "for whites only" in midtown Manhattan.

Mercer Ellington later recalled that when he visited his parents in 1924, the three of them slept in one small room. There was a couch for him and a double bed for them. Mercer's memoirs say: "In the apartment there was no front room, playroom or anything like that. All the space, including the living and dining rooms, was rented except the kitchen and the bathroom. I can remember Mr. Leonard Harper's apartment vividly, in the heart of Harlem, at 2067 Seventh Avenue. I recall going around the corner and up the street to Weisbecker's when I was 5 years old to get hot dogs and sardine sandwiches for breakfast... I was always the first one to awaken because my dad and mother were night people and that is why I generally took care of myself and got my first meal of the day independently."

A nationally popular dancer and nite club producer, Leonard Harper and Joe Louis, the World Heavyweight Champion, had a dancing act for a brief period after WWII.

In March, 1924, leader-banjoist Elmer Snowden left the band and Duke Ellington took over leadership of the Washingtonians. The changing of the musical guard did not rate any attention from entertainment reporters. Newspaper writers focused their attention on the changing roster of singers, dancers and comedians. Leonard Harper's All Colored Dixie Revue, however would occasionally get a mention in both Variety and Billboard, the two major entertainment weeklies. Newspapers paid absolutely no attention to Ellington's Washingtonians, although they were the sole feature at the Kentucky Club (Holiday Cafe) until midnight. At the stroke of 12, Harper's Dixie Revue would go on, accompanied by the Washingtonians, and then do a second show at 2 a.m.

Approximately a year after Ellington assumed the leadership of the band, the press began taking notice with such statements as "The Washingtonians are the hottest band this side of the equator." Another reporter wrote, "If anybody can tell us where a hotter aggregation than Duke Ellington and his Kentucky Club Serenaders can be found, we will buy for the mob." That statement takes on real significance when one considers that during the Prohibition period, between 1920 and 1933, the mob controlled the bootleg whiskey and speakeasy operations throughout the United States.

Duke Ellington's aggregation worked at the off-Broadway Kentucky Club (formerly the Hollywood Cafe) for four years. Ellington remembers: "It was a good place for us to be because it stayed open all night and became a rendezvous for all the big time stars and musicians on Broadway after they got through working. Paul Whiteman came in often, and he always showed his appreciation by laying a big fifty dollar tip on us." It was at the Kentucky Club that Duke Ellington and his Serenaders began creating musical sounds that would later be marketed to attract the thrill-seeking bejeweled flappers and their escorts wearing top hats and black ties. The Park Avenue and Broadway bunch flocked into the club to hear Ellington's unadulterated sensual music style. New, haunting sounds of the Ellingtonians were the direct result of unanticipated changes in

James Wesley "Bubber" Miley, the dean of the plunger mute trumpet soloist, worked with Duke from September 1923 until January 1929. He died in Welfare Island, N.Y. in May 1932 at age 29.

the band's personnel. Arthur Whetsol left the aggregation to complete his studies at Howard University in Washington to be replaced by "Bubber" Miley, the dean of the plunger mute trumpet soloists. His horn spoke in a primitive language and told stories that only the truly initiated could understand. Those who came within the sound waves of his horn believed everything it said. The "Bubber" Miley experience penetrated the depth of the soul and

22

Irving Mills, Ellington's financial manager and promoter.

was a major influence on what became known as the Ellington sound. Duke Ellington's "East St. Louis Toodle-O," a musical portrait of Bubber's work, foretold what was to come.

Joe "Tricky Sam" Nanton replaced Charley Irvis on trombone. Irvis left the Duke on October 22,1925, to join the very popular, red hot and low down Charlie Johnson's Orchestra at Small's Paradise Club at 135th Street and Seventh Avenue in Harlem. "Tricky Sam" and "Bubber" Miley complemented each other in that both were expert at creating animalistic growl sounds with mutes and plungers. Musical conversations emanating from their horns frequently left Kentucky Club listeners spellbound.

Irving Mills, a music publisher and talented four-corner hustler, was a regular customer at the Kentucky Club. He had an ear for the musically unusual. Duke and his men were music makers with a different sound. One night Mills made known his wishes to record the band and Ellington jumped at the opportunity.

On November 29,1926, Mills arranged for the band's first transcriptions on the Vocalion label. Ellington recorded four of his own compositions, including "East St. Louis Toodle-O" and "Birmingham Breakdown." Mills also had them record the same numbers on different labels, giving the band a different name on each one. It was the Duke Ellington Orchestra on Victor label, the Jungle Band on Brunswick, the Washingtonians on the Harmony label and the Harlem Foot Warmers on Okeh label. Mills also had them record under the names of different sidemen in the orchestra, including Sonny Greer and His Memphis Men. Recording opportunities gave the Ellington band a spectacular lift in popularity.

Shortly before the Christmas, 1926, Irving Mills began working as Ellington's manager. He secured playing dates and national media coverage, as well as music publishing opportunities. Mills always cut himself in for co-author credits, though he never wrote a single note.

In addition to his opportunistic business skills, Irving Mills was a natural born publicity agent. He reached the ears and eyes of power brokers in the music industry and initially treated Ellington with the respect reserved for maestros, demanding that others treat the Duke with similar deference.

Duke's musical reputation spread quickly across the landscape and particularly in Chicago by Erskine Tate, Dave Peyton, Clarence Black and Carroll Dickerson, all popular and talented colored orchestra leaders.

The Duke, with Mills' guidance, was rapidly becoming the king of the musical hill, threatening the pre-eminence that Fletcher Henderson had enjoyed for several years. The true identity of the reigning monarch of the Jazz Age became obvious when Duke Ellington ascended the musical throne at the world famous Cotton Club on December 4,1927.

The original Cotton Club at Lenox and 145th Street in Harlem in 1927.

4 - THE JAZZ SLAVE MASTERS

The mob-controlled Cotton Club was operated by 20th century slave masters. Talented jazz musicians were chained to specific night clubs and saloons in the North in the same manner as slaves were shackled to the large cotton and tobacco plantations in the antebellum South. Duke Ellington, Louis Armstrong, Cab Calloway, Earl Hines, Jimmie Lunceford and many others were inmates behind the "Cotton Curtain" at various periods in their careers from 1924 to 1941 and beyond.

"Hi De Ho Man" Cab Calloway, whose name was synonymous with the Cotton Club.

The Jimmie Lunceford Jazz Express followed the Calloway Orchestra into the Cotton Club.

The bandstand at the Harlem Cotton Club was a replica of an antebellum Southern mansion with large white fluted columns evenly spaced across the veranda. The backdrop of the stage was painted with weeping willows and slave quarters. The orchestra performed in front of the large double doors to the "mansion."

Down four steps was the dance floor where floor shows took place. In every show chorus girls performed at least one semi-nude jungle number, Waiters were dressed in red tuxedos in the style of butlers in a Southern mansion, and tables were covered with red and white checkered gingham tablecloths. The entire scene created a "Gone With the Wind" atmosphere that made every white male feel like Rhett Butler and every white woman Scarlett O'Hara. Since the waiters were paid only $1 a night, they had to hustle like sky caps and hope that Rhett Butler would drop a big tip.

The half naked Cotton Club chorus girls doing their stuff. Ellington Orchestra is playing a jungle number in the background.

The Boss Slave Master at the Cotton Club was Owney Madden, one of the most notorious prohibition bootleggers. In Chicago the Slave Master was Al Capone. Johnny Lazia controlled the police, liquor and gambling in Kansas City and the Purple Gang controlled the booze, dives and girls in Detroit.

Money was what the plantation system was all about. The Grand Terrace in Chicago, the most grandiose plantation in the country, had decor more elaborate than New York's Cotton Club. Everything and everybody in the club smelled like new money except the colored entertainers who were all sweating black teardrops, earning pittances and smiling to masquerade their grief. Earl Hines, internationally renowned pianist and Grand Terrace bandleader, did not escape the lashes of the Slave Master.

Owney Madden, boot legger and New York City jazz slave master.

Al Capone, jazz slave master and King of Chicago's South Side bootleg operations.

The original Grand Terrace at 39th & South Parkway in Chicago, officially opened on December 28, 1928 featuring the Earl Hines Orchestra and a girlie show. This picture was taken in 1983.

The Hines Orchestra's star trumpet and saxophone player, George Dixon, was naive in the ways that the mob's plantation system worked. He decided to better his lot in life and give Earl Hines the standard two-week notice before leaving to join Don Redman's band in Detroit. Redman formerly was the brilliant arranger with the Fletcher Henderson Orchestra and music director of the famous McKinney's Cotton Pickers Orchestra. Redman was interested in having Omer Simeon, Hines's alto sax man, and Billy Franklin, the trombonist, join Dixon in his move to Detroit to become members of his new band.

The famous Don Redman Orchestra at Connie's Inn in Harlem in 1932.

Dixon told the writer, "The day we left Chicago, Ralph Cooper, producer of the show at the original Grand Terrace, came out of the club and shook our hands while we were standing near the curb of the inner drive on South Parkway (now Martin Luther King Drive). When I stepped into my little 1929 Ford and said 'Goodbye,' Cooper replied, 'I am not going to say goodbye because you'll be back.'

"I said, 'Not a chance.'

"Shortly after we arrived in Detroit, Don called his first rehearsal at the Graystone Ballroom. Before we could play the first note, Don's manager came up and asked, 'Where's the three fellows from Earl Hines's band?'

"We all raised our hands and identified ourselves. Don's manager said,

"'Well, I just got a call from New York and I won't be able to use

Ralph Cooper, dancer and producer of the Grand Terrace Floor Show.

you guys.'

"The three of us yelled in unison, 'Does that mean we have to go back to Chicago?'

"The manager replied, 'Yeah, that's what it means.'

"After hearing that bad news, the three of us jumped into my little Ford and headed back to the Windy City. The mob, through intimidation and organization, had things so well-regulated we couldn't even change jobs."

Some weeks later, Dixon happened to overhear a conversation between Ed Fox, Capone's manager at the Grand Terrace, and Frank "The Enforcer" Nitti, a Capone henchman, that shed light on their Detroit experience. It seemed that Joe Fusco, Al Capone's superintendent of breweries, who was also one of the plantation overseers at the Grand Terrace, had called Owney Madden, the mob leader who owned the Cotton Club in New York, and told him that George Dixon and several sidemen had left Hines and he wanted them to return to the Grand Terrace in Chicago. Madden immediately called the leader of the Purple Gang in Detroit, and that individual gave the word directly to Don Redman's manager that the boys had to return to Chicago. The "word" from the Jazz Slave Masters was always the final message.

Cab Calloway, who toiled under the same system, was once threatened with violence by Owney Madden's mob if he didn't act right. Calloway was working and broadcasting from Madden's New York Cotton Club and his popularity was soaring. The mob arranged to book him and his band into the Paramount Theater in midtown New York for a three-week engagement without adding any additional money to their Cotton Club salaries. Cab became obstinate and fighting mad about doubling on two gigs for the same dollars.

Cab was told in no uncertain terms: "You'd better go into the Paramount and be happy or we'll see to it that you never work again."

With that message clanging in his ears, Cab 'hi-de-ho'd and he-de-ha'd' to both his midtown gig at the Paramount and to his uptown gig at Harlem's Cotton Club for three consecutive weeks. Needless to say, he was not late for a single performance.

Dempsey J. Travis, the author, interviewing Earl Hines in August 1983.

The New York Jazz Slave Masters had long arms that frequently reached into Chicago to protect their chattels. Duke Ellington recalls an experience when he was scheduled for an engagement at the Paradise Theater on Chicago's West Side. When he arrived at the theater the manager, Sam Fletcher, told Duke that some members of a West Side mob had been there that morning and said that Duke had to send them $500 or he wouldn't leave the theater alive that night. Duke immediately called Owney Madden at the Cotton Club in New York and told him what had happened. Madden said: "Duke, don't worry about it. I can assure you that you won't have any trouble."

After reassuring Duke, Owney Madden grabbed the phone again within minutes to call Al Capone in Chicago to tell him about Duke's troubles with the West Side hoodlums. Capone immediately issued the following order: "Duke Ellington is not to be bothered on the West Side or in the Loop." Duke later said, "Those words closed the chapter on the gangster problem for me and the band in Chicago from that day forward."

Al Capone saved Duke Ellington from threats of violence, but chained Earl Hines to a $150-a-week contract constructed to last forever. Ed Fox, Capone's front man and the Grand Terrace manager, had a contract with Hines that literally would not permit Hines to use his own name if he attempted to leave the Grand Terrace plantation. His contract was in perpetuity: If Ed Fox died, Hines would become the personal property of Fox's widow, and in the event of her death, Fox's elder son would be heir to the contract for his lifetime. If the oldest son died before Hines, the contract would pass to Fox's younger son. This chattel contract on Earl Hines was in effect from December, 1928, until a March, 1941, engagement at the Regal Theater in Chicago where Hines gathered his music after the last show and told the band:

Harry Gray, the fearless president of Local 208.

"I am not working for Ed Fox anymore."

Hines had made this threat before, but this time he apparently intended to keep his word.

Early the following Monday, Hines and George Dixon, his saxophone and trumpet player, went to Harry Gray, president of Local 208, at 3934 South State Street, headquarters of the Colored Musicians' Union in Chicago. Hines told Gray his story and Gray called James C. (Jimmy) Petrillo, president of the National Federation of Musicians in New York. Petrillo was also president of Local 10, the Chicago downtown union for white musicians.

Petrillo came into town that Wednesday and met with Harry Gray, Earl Hines, Charlie Carpenter and George Dixon at the Palmer House in downtown Chicago.

According to Dixon, Petrillo read the contract and said,"This contract is not worth the paper it is written on. It's too much Ed Fox and not enough Earl Hines, so you go and work anywhere you want for anyone you want and I will protect you."

Dixon remembered that Fox did not relinquish Hines even after the powerful Jimmy Petrillo had told Hines he was free. Shortly after his emancipation, Hines took a band into New York's Apollo Theater. Fox immediately procured an injunction through his New

York lawyers and tied up the band's weekly salary. When Petrillo got this news he called Jack Schiffman, manager of the Apollo, and told him, "If you don't release the band's payroll, your show will not go on tonight!" Jack Schiffman immediately responded by releasing the payroll.

George Dixon, the straw boss of the Earl Hines Orchestra. Dixon joined the Hines Orchestra on May 15, 1930, and stayed until he joined the Navy in September, 1942.

Although jazz is music known for its free forum, the colored people who played it were never free agents. Owney Madden once told Duke Ellington that he would never be free to leave the New York Cotton Club plantation unless he agreed to pay the orchestra that replaced him out of money that Ellington earned on his road tours. Duke's road trips would vary from two weeks to three months, depending upon the nature of the engagements. Sometimes the gigs were extended theater tours; others could be 14-day movie assignments in Hollywood. The Ellington band's first replacement was the Missourians with Cab Calloway fronting the unit. Duke paid Cab $200 a week to conduct and act as the master of ceremonies.

The actual choice of Cab and the Missourians was made by the Cotton Club mob. Gangsters simply took control of Cab and his band from a white booking agent named Moe Gale with pure muscle and threats to the agent's health. The mob closed the deal for Calloway's services by kissing Gale on the left cheek and offering him 10% of Cab Calloway's annual earnings.

Duke Ellington's 1930 Cotton Club Band

The Ellington and Calloway Cotton Club venture was ultimately structured to give Duke and Irving Mills, song publisher and booking agent, 50% of Cab Calloway Enterprises. In addition, Mills owned 50% of Duke Ellington Inc. In the postwar period, the Jazz Slave Masters permitted some serfs to own at least 50% of themselves. But remember, the Jazz Slave Masters always controlled the cash register, paid the piper and called the tune.

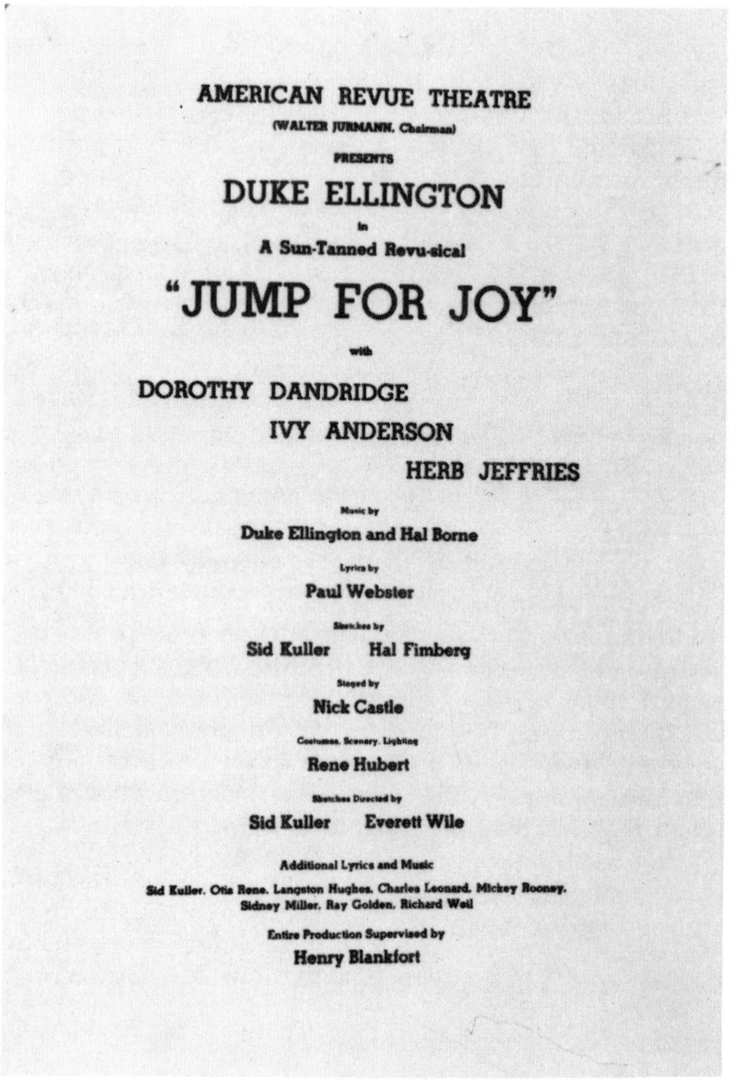

AMERICAN REVUE THEATRE

(WALTER JURMANN, Chairman)

PRESENTS

DUKE ELLINGTON

In

A Sun-Tanned Revu-sical

"JUMP FOR JOY"

with

DOROTHY DANDRIDGE

IVY ANDERSON

HERB JEFFRIES

Music by

Duke Ellington and Hal Borne

Lyrics by

Paul Webster

Sketches by

Sid Kuller   Hal Fimberg

Staged by

Nick Castle

Costumes, Scenery, Lighting

Rene Hubert

Sketches Directed by

Sid Kuller   Everett Wile

Additional Lyrics and Music

Sid Kuller, Otis Rene, Langston Hughes, Charles Leonard, Mickey Rooney,
Sidney Miller, Ray Golden, Richard Weil

Entire Production Supervised by

Henry Blankfort

5 - THEY JUMPED FOR JOY

In August of 1930, the Duke Ellington Orchestra traveled to the West Coast by train to do some guest shots in "Check and Double Check," a film featuring the popular radio team of Amos 'N' Andy. During the late 1920's and early 30's, the Andy 'N' Amos program was the most listened to show in the United States. It dominated the country's listening habits in the 48 states for 15 minutes five nights a week. George Bernard Shaw, the Irish-born, Nobel Prize winner for literature, measured the comedians' impact when he said: "Three things I shall never forget about America - the Rocky Mountains, Niagara Falls and Amos 'N' Andy."

George Bernad Shaw, Nobel Prize Winner and author of Pygmalion (1913) and Saint Joan (1923).

Among musical numbers the Ellington Orchestra played in the film were "The Mystery Song," "East St. Louis Toodle-O," "Old Man Blues," "Three Little Words," and "Ring Dem Bells." The latter two songs became hits shortly after the movie was released. The syncopated tunes have subsequently become big dance band standards.

Duke termed his appearance in the film a "crowning point." His Negro fans and many white liberals did not share his opinion because they felt that the enormously talented and articulate musician deserved more than five brief flashes across the big screen. Moreover, his presence in the film was blacked out of the news releases and on all the theater marquees in the country except those in the most sophisticated Northern urban areas. The RKO Studio executives feared that spotlighting a Negro would offend Southern movie goers.

Negroes generally enjoyed the humor of "Amos 'N' Andy" on the radio in the privacy of their homes. However, the movie was unlike the radio in that you saw with your naked eyes Charles Correll and Freeman Gosden, two white men masquerading across the screen as Negroes. They wore several layers of burnt cork on their faces in addition to exaggeratedly big lips painted white. Radio, unlike the movie, was not as offensive in that it forced the listeners to employ their imaginations and mirror through the mind's eye two Negro comedians actually playing those hilariously funny roles.

A snapshot of the Ellington brass section in the movie "Check and Double Check." Standing left are Joe"Tricky Sam" Nanton and Juan Tizol in black face because the producer did not want him to appear white. Seated left are Freddy Jenkins, Cootie Williams, and Art Whetsol.

As the swing era reached its peak in the mid-30's, Hollywood developed a separate platform for Negro performers in keeping with the Jim Crow mind-set for presenting popular Negro entertainers without making them a part of the plot. Moreover, there was an absence of intelligent dialogue written in movie scripts for Negroes, that is, unless they were wearing a maid's apron or a coachman's cap. There was also a special language for sharecroppers whose bodies were always draped in blue overalls or colorful gingham dresses, complemented with red or blue bandannas around their necks or on their heads. Duke Ellington and members of his band were not forced to dress down from their customary elegance, a compromise that gave artistic dignity to the musician. In that sense, Duke was right in calling it a "crowning point."

A publicity shot of Duke being chased by the ladies on the Hollywood lot of R.K.O. pictures.

The Ellington men actually raised the dressing bar for Negroes in the movies following their appearance in "Amos 'N' Andy" wearing black tuxedos and not having to scratch where they did not itch. In their next major film, "Belle of the 90's," done in 1934 and featuring Mae West, the orchestra was decked out in white formals while playing a swinging Ellington arrangement of "Ebony Rhapsody" based on Franz Liszt's "Second Hungarian Rhapsody." The movie's ebony audiences applauded the Ellington men as if they had given a live performance. Witnessing and participating in this event gave the author, then a young jazz piano player, a feeling of cultural emancipation.

Between 1930 and 1941 the Duke Ellington Orchestra appeared in seven major movies and three five-minute shorts. It was in the early summer of 1941 that Duke reached his theatrical "Pikes Peak" in that he and Billy Strayhorn wrote the entire music score for a Sun-Tanned Revu-sical entitled "Jump For Joy" featuring Dorothy Dandridge, Ivie Anderson, Herb Jeffries and the Duke as both actor and musician. The spirited title song contained these lines:

"Don't you grieve, Little Eve,
All the hounds, I do believe
Have been killed, ain't you thrilled,
Jump for joy."

The idea for the "Jump For Joy" production was a collaborative effort of 15 Hollywood screen writers, including Mickey Rooney, the movie star, and Langston Hughes, the great Negro poet. They decided they would attempt to eliminate racism in America through a form of theatrical propaganda. The original script had Uncle Tom on his death bed with all of his children dancing around him singing, "He lived to a ripe old age. Let him go, God bless him!" At the same time, there was a Hollywood producer on the left side of the bed and a Broadway producer on the right side, both trying to keep Uncle Tom alive by injecting adrenaline into the veins of his arms.

The opening act was entitled "Sun Tan Tenth of a Nation!" and the finale of the first act was "Uncle Tom's Cabin Is a Drive-In Now!" The first eight bars of the lyrics were:

> "There used to be a chicken shack in Caroline,
> But now they've moved it to Hollywood and Vine;
> They paid off the mortgage - nobody knows how-
> And Uncle Tom's Cabin is a drive-in now!"

Ellington said that the "angels" (investors) made them take out the original second act of the show because it had more fishbones than America was willing to swallow. It was called "I've Got A

This poster advertises a 19-minute film made in 1929 to publicize the band. The plot involved a band rehearsal and the simulated death of singer Fredi Washington.

Passport From Georgia (And I'm Going to the U.S.A.)"

The "Jump For Joy" revue opened July 10, 1941, at the Mayan Theater in Los Angeles and closed 12 weeks later on September 27 following a highly successful run. The initial objective was to take the show across the country from Los Angeles to San Francisco, Chicago, Boston and then to Broadway. The message was too strong for anti-fascist and anti-Nazi pre-World War II America. Therefore, financing for the show dried up like a grape in the sun. The show never played anywhere outside of Los Angeles,

Jimmy Blanton and Duke Ellington look on as Herb Jeffries sings one of the "Jump For Joy" title songs from the orchestra pit of Mayan Theater in Los Angeles.

except for a three-week aborted revival in 1958 in Miami.

Ellington made this observation about "Jump For Joy": "The audience itself was of unusual composition, for it included the most celebrated Hollywoodians, middle-class ofays (whites), the sweet-and-low, scuffling-type Negroes, and also dicty Negroes (doctors, lawyers and the like). After seeing the show, Negroes left the theater feeling proud, with their chests sticking out and "Jumping for Joy."

Duke Ellington and his father, James Edward Ellington, detraining at the Dearborn Street Station in Chicago. A Pullman porter is shown in the background.

6 - RIDING THE "A TRAIN" UPTOWN AND BEYOND

The Duke Ellington Orchestra left the East Coast by train enroute to the West Coast in the late summer of 1930. They stopped over in Chicago to play a one-night dance engagement at the beautiful Savoy Ballroom which had opened its doors on Thanksgiving Day, November 24, 1927, at 47th Street and South Parkway (Martin Luther King Drive). The street became known as the America Sepia Broadway because the Regal Theater opened next door to the Savoy Ballroom on February 4,1928, adding to an existing entertainment milieu that included the Owl Theater, Apollo Theater, Metropolitan Theater, Warrick Hall and the Roseland Ballroom.

Chicago's Savoy Ballroom at 47th and South Parkway could accommo-date 3,600 dancers.

42

Duke described pre-Depression Chicago as being more awesome than the glittering, glamorous place he had envisioned while eavesdropping on waiters' and Pullman porters' conversations about "Chi-kor-ga" in Frank Holliday's Washington poolroom during his wild teenage years.

The Ellington band returned to Chicago on February 12,1931, after appearing at Boston's Metropolitan Theater for a week. The

band opened on Friday, February 13,1931-the Duke's favorite day-at the Oriental Theater,on Randolph Street near State Street in downtown Chicago. Ivie Anderson, a girl from Gilroy, California, was hired by the Duke for the Oriental gig after she had been recommended by Earl Hines. Ellington had seen her perform in Earl Hines's Revue at the Grand Terrace nite club when he stopped over in Chicago in August of 1930. The Grand Terrace was a mob-controlled speakeasy that catered primarily to white folk, although it was located on the South Side of Chicago in the heart of the "Black Belt." Ivie was a multi-talented entertainer with a malted-milk complexion. In addition to being a top-flight singer in the class of

Oriental Theater in Chicago

such stars as Bessie Smith, Ethel Waters and Adelaide Hall, she was also a professional dancer and comedienne. Duke considered her his good-luck charm because her act enabled the Ellington group to break the Oriental Theater's all-time attendance record.

In addition to Ivie Anderson's show-stopping performance, Johnny Hodges from Boston was not "short-stopping" when he matched her act by making his soprano saxophone figuratively weep as he played the "Rent Party Blues." Then "Cootie" Williams, a Mobile, Alabama, boy, came center stage, rhythmically twisting his body, distorting his face and closing his eyes as he barked "Black and Tan Fantasy" through the bell of his trumpet. Bringing up the rear in that set was Joe "Tricky Sam" Nanton of New York

City, who lifted theater goers into a state of disbelief with his trombone "yah-yahing" a talking rendition of "Jazz Lips."

By popular demand, the Ellington troupe returned to the Oriental Theater the following month. This time Duke, who was very superstitious, insisted on opening on Friday, March 13th, because he now believed that Friday the Thirteenth was his lucky day. Validity of his superstition was seemingly confirmed when the Ellingtonians' second appearance at the Oriental broke the previous all-time attendance record at the Balaban & Katz movie and vaudeville palace.

Ivie Anderson, a world class singer and entertainer.

Irving Mills had negotiated a contract with Balaban & Katz, the theater moguls, for Ellington to play in all of their major Chicago vaudeville houses for eight consecutive weeks. Eight weeks gave Ellington ample opportunity to both see and smell Carl Sandburg's city with the big shoulders.

After a month in the city that Sandburg had poetically labeled "Hog Butcher For The World" Duke made the following observation: "The most impressive aspect of Chicago was that the South Side (Bronzeville) was together. It was a us-for-we, we-for-us community. It was a community with 12 Negro millionaires, no hungry Negroes, no complaining Negroes, no crying Negroes, and no Uncle Tom Negroes..." Among the 12 millionaires that Duke mentioned, and he missed some, were: Robert Abbott, the Chicago Defender publisher; Anthony Overton, the banker and cosmetics manufacturer; the Sewell brothers, heirs to an oil fortune, Illy Kelly and his brothers, Walter and Ross; Edward Jones and his brothers, George and McKissick; "Big Jim" Martin; "Pop" Lewis; "Giver Dam" Jones and his brother, Teenan.

At age 11 the author was taken by his mother, Mrs. Mittie Travis, on a trip downtown on the streetcar-known in the 'hood as "Big Red" to see Duke Ellington at the magnificent Oriental Theater. I recall we arrived at the theater on Saturday, February 14,1931, at

The Duke Ellington Primer

The Ellington Orchestra on stage at the Oriental Theater. Seated left to right: Harry Carney, Johnny Hodges, Barney Bigard, Fred Guy and Duke. Standing: 2nd Row: Wellman Braud, seated at piano, and Sonny Greer. 3rd Row: Freddy Jenkins, "Cootie" Williams, Juan Tizol and Joe Nanton.

Robert S. Abbott, millionaire publisher of Chicago Defender.

8:45 a.m. to guarantee that we would be able to buy two early-bird tickets that cost 35 cents until noon. The grand cost for a glorious day of entertainment for two, including transportation on the trolley and two Baby Ruth candy bars, was $1.

Both my mother and father, Louis Travis, were eager that I see and hear Duke Ellington with the expectation that the experience would inspire me to take more interest in my piano lessons. They hoped that I would become a band leader someday instead of a laborer in the stockyards or in the steel mills where most Negroes worked.

The grand idea of becoming a great band leader, like Ellington,

Johnny Sewell, in 1937, is shown standing by his futuristic car parked in front of Joe's Deluxe Club at 63rd and South Park in Chicago.

George Jones, Policy Baron

McKissick Jones, A Policy King

wore well in developing my self esteem for several years. Then I heard Nat "King" Cole, a fellow student at Wendell Phillips High School, and his Twelve Dukes at the Warwick Hall on Easter

46

Sunday in 1934. Nat was only three years older than , but he and his 12 piece band of teenagers sounded exactly like the great Earl "Father" Hines Orchestra I had heard many times broadcasting from the Grand Terrace nite club. The piano skills of both Hines and Cole melted my vision of ever becoming a great piano player. With that mind-set, my fantasy of ever being a top-rate ivory plucker faded like smoke rings blown through the lips of a beautiful girl.

Seconds after my mother purchased our Oriental Theater tickets, we were standing in the grand foyer. The theater was best described in the December 25,1926, edition of the Motion Picture News Journal: "The theater was a flawless example of the best in Oriental art, including the entresol floor and balcony, with a

The foyer of the Oriental Theater

capacity of about 4,000 seats. The exterior of the entrance is unusually interesting with the East Indian ornament and grotesques around the large window over the sheltering canopy, giving the effect of a grand triumphal arch—the entrance to the Orient. The interior surpasses anything heretofore attempted for a place of amusement of this character. It is an educational treat in itself as a work of art to study and examine the array of sculptured detail throughout the theater. The entrance or grand lobby is elaborately treated with marble columns and walls extending 40 feet high and enriched with ornamental plaster panels, mosaic glass niches, and overhead balconies in the architecture of the Far East Orient and brilliantly illuminated with special lighting effects. Imported mosaic glasslined niches in the upper side wall bays of this lobby are of most interesting original Indian design, depicting dancers of the Orient and are examples of the highest class of mosaic art. The massive ceiling beams and enclosing ceiling panels and coffers are richly ornamented on all surfaces with a multitude of varying Oriental detail. The main cornice frieze is formed with a series of recessed niches in which are located concealed electric lights. Marble stairs lead up from either side of this

lobby to the entresol foyer above, meeting on and forming a balcony at the north end of the lobby. Another balcony occurs at the
front or opposite end of the lobby..."

A view of Ellington at work from the wings of the Oriental Theater.

The splendor of the theater auditorium was overshadowed by the
sound of Duke Ellington's music. Soft red lights made the
Ellingtonians barely visible behind the thin cotton scrim as the
band opened the vaudeville section of the show by playing the
mournful sounds of "East St. Louis Toodle-O," Ellington's signa-
ture theme. Strains of the"Toodle-O" haunting melody floated

through the theater like a perfume mist. Before you could recover from the initial impact of the smell, taste and sound of his theme song, a blue spotlight beamed down from the ceiling silhouetting Duke at the piano playing a short overture of several of his popular compositions. At this point, the audience broke into loud spontaneous applause. Just before the applause subsided, Ivie Anderson appeared stage left, in back of the scrim under an orange spotlight, wearing a dazzling white gown, singing and dancing to an abridged version of "Doin' the Crazy Walk." Johnny Hodges was subsequently seen stage right, behind the scrim, blowing several bars of "Mood Indigo." The scrim disappears, the lights go up, the orchestra bandstand moves forward and Duke steps out to the footlights to take a bow and greet the cheering crowd as the band plays "Rockin' in Rhythm," a 1931 Ellington composition. The audience reacted to the musical excitement with stomping feet and thunderous applause. The show was on!

Ivie Anderson broke up the house singing, dancing and cracking jokes with Sonny Greer, the drummer and her straight man. After her performance, she was forced to return to the center stage four times for encores. Ivie Anderson ultimately had to make a speech to cool the house down. The Chicago music critics gave the Ellington production rave reviews. The only negative was that the 45-minute show had moved at such a fast pace, it seemed like 10 minutes as opposed to three quarters of an hour. Downtown Chicago just could not get its fill of Duke Ellington so he had to return to the Oriental Theater five times in 1931 and fans were still thirsty for more.

The South Side Bronzevillians wanted to touch the hem of Ellington's garment on their own political turf, just as the downtown natives had. Therefore, the Duke followed his Oriental opening with a week-long engagement at the Regal Theater, at 47th Street and South Parkway (Martin Luther King Drive), beginning on February 20,1931. It was a history making week for show business in the Negro community. Acts accompanying Duke at the Regal were Ivie Anderson; the Four Blazers, who had worked with him for three years at the Cotton Club, and the Lovely Regalettes dancing chorus line.

South Siders came in herds to see and hear Duke Ellington, the uncrowned authentic King of Jazz. Sepia and white jazz patrons waited for hours in lines four abreast, lines that snaked around the block and moved at a snail's pace when they moved at all. A revolving crowd stood patiently waiting for the first, second, third and fourth shows to let out. Fans who were lucky and patient would gain entry to the lobby where they might stand for another hour with 1,500 other theater goers. Admittance to the lobby was a guarantee that you would occupy one of the 3,500 plush red seats during the next theater break. The exact number of seats available was not certain because some individuals, like the writer, would sit through two or three Ellington productions without ever permitting the seat to get cold.

The Regal Theater and Savoy Ballroom complex - the center of the Negro Broadway in Chicago during 1930's and 1940's.

The wait to get into the theater was always well worth the time to hear Duke play "Black Beauty," written by Ellington in 1928 and dedicated to the memory of Florence Mills, one of New York Broadway's first Negro singing and dancing stars. "The Mooch," another staple that Duke frequently played from his 1929 song book, was one of those finger tingling, spine chilling exotic jungle numbers that Ellington and some members of his orchestra collectively invented.

To date there has not been another orchestra, black or white, that could duplicate the Ellington sound, although many have tried, including the Stan Kenton Orchestra , the Woody Herman Herd and the Charlie Barnet Band.

Barnet, the son of a very wealthy family, constantly bolsted Duke's ego by playing from a book crowded with Ellington com-

A lobby scene of the Regal Theater

positions. He even hired the Ellington band to play for his private parties. To his credit, Barnet did not suffer from what Duke called the "skin disease." He employed Negroes like Lena Horne in 1941; "Peanuts" Holland, trumpet, in 1942; and Howard McGee, trumpet, James "Trummy" Young, trombone, and Oscar Pettiford on bass in 1943.

On the other hand, Stan Kenton wanted to be a white Jimmie Lunceford since it was impossible to be another Duke Ellington in any color. Moreover, the early Lunceford Orchestra combined the influences of both Ellington and Louis Armstrong in some of their arrangements.

After completing the Regal Theater gig, Ellington played a week-long engagement at the Uptown Theater on the North Side and then the Paradise Theater on the West Side. From there the orchestra went to Detroit, Omaha, Minneapolis, Des Moines, Denver, Kansas City, St. Louis, Indianapolis, back to Chicago, Toronto, Cleveland, again back to Chicago, Cincinnati, Pittsburgh, Philadelphia and Washington.

Weekly theater dates of the 1930's were like holidays compared to the one-night dance gigs and concert dates that kept the band

Charlie Barnet and his Orchestra featuring Herbert "Peanuts" Holland on trumpet.

The popular counter sheet music for "It Don't Mean A Thing."

on the road 52 weeks a year for almost 40 years. The exception was when the gigs dried up because of the economy or changes in popular musical taste. During those periods, Duke kept the band intact by maintaining the weekly payroll for his men from his ASCAP fees and the royalties from his compositions.

Duke Ellington's 1932 traveling circuit did not vary a great deal from 1931, except that he added five new compositions to his song book, including a great standard made famous by Ivie Anderson called "It Don't Mean A Thing If You Ain't Got That Swing." And, man, could she swing!

The Ellington entourage of 18 musicians and entertainers, moments after disembarking at Southampton, England, on June 9, 1933.

7 - The Brits And Parisians Meet The Duke

Ellington and an entourage of 18 musicians and entertainers sailed from the port of New York on June 3, 1933, on the luxurious Olympic ocean liner en route to England. During the transatlantic trip they played an unscheduled concert for the ship's passengers. As a result of the impromptu jam session, men of the orchestra made many new friends during the voyage.

All members of the orchestra enjoyed the ocean trip except Duke who had an unreasoning fear of being shipwrecked. His superstition about ships could be traced directly to a story his mother told him about her experience on a ship when she was pregnant. Duke's nights on the ship were spent nervously playing cards and drinking.

When members of the band and the entertainers disembarked at Southampton, England, on Friday, June 9, just after noon, they quickly discovered that no decent hotel would rent them lodging because of the color of their skin. These social lepers were the same individuals who later the same day were to be greeted like royalty by 37 reporters and photographers at London's Waterloo train station.

The housing accommodation problem was resolved by the group splitting up and seeking accommodations at assorted Bloomsbury hotels and rooming houses. Individuals living in the Bloomsbury residential section of North-Central London were considered liberal because of their intellectual attitude about race. In that area there were such luminaries as Virginia Woolf, E. M. Forster and John Maynard Keynes. However, the general housing segregation pattern in Great Britain was not unlike the "Black Belt" pattern imposed by their American cousins.

The Duke Ellington organization began its stay in Great Britain with a two-week gig at the Palladium in London on June 12. Although the show started at 6:30 p.m., Duke and his people did not go on until after 8 p.m. Ellington was the last act of the evening and number 13 on the program, a place the superstitious Duke may have appreciated.

"Spike" Hughes, a musician and music critic for Melody Maker

The Duke Ellington Primer

Virginia Woolf, English novelist and critic. Her works include "Night And Day" (1919), "Jacob's Room" (1922), "Mrs. Dolloway "(1925), "The Waves" (1931).

Magazine, was present at the opening and observed: "When No. 13 went up on the board the applause grew into a roar, the pit orchestra faded out, and we heard-for the first time in England-the magic sound of Duke Ellington and his famous orchestra. The curtain went up and there they were! Even the six brass were inaudible amidst the thunder of applause. Duke, sitting in the centre of the band down stage at the piano, with his back half-turned to the audience, looked over his shoulder and smiled and bowed to the tumultuous reception.

"The band was dressed in pearl-grey tail suits, the Duke himself in a double-breasted lounge suit of the same color and a bright orange tie. On Duke's left were the three trumpets, on his right four saxophones; behind the trumpets, on a higher rostrum, were the three trombones; behind the saxes were the bass and banjo; and high up at the back was Sonny Greer, the drummer.

"There they all were, the names we have met so often in the Gramophone Review: (Saxes) Barney Bigard, Johnny Hodges, Harry Carney, Otto Hardwick (misspelt on the programme "Ottox"!) (trumpets) Arty Whetsel (misspelt on the programme "Whetsol"), Charlie [Cootie] Williams, Fred Jenkins; (trombones) Lawrence Brown, Juan Tizol, Joe Nanton; (bass) William [recte Wellman] Braud (a spelling error on program); (banjo) Fred Guy; and (drums) Sonny Greer. When the applause subsided a little I discovered that the band was playing 'Ring Dem Bells,' mostly as the record.

John Maynard Keynes, English economist, his work includes "Economic Consequences of Peace" (1919) and "Treatise on Money" (1930).

"They finished with a sudden and unexpected coda; Duke jumped from his seat and walked to the footlights. It was minutes before he could make himself heard. He and the boys seemed overwhelmed by the reception.

"Then they played 'Three Little Words,' then 'Stormy Weather,' which Ivie Anderson sang. Then followed an encore by Miss Anderson, 'Give Me A Man Like That' [recte 'I Want A Man Like That']. Then an old favorite -'Bugle Call Rag.'

"It is useless for me to attempt to describe each number separately. You all know how Ellington's band plays through listening to his records, and I can only say that, in the flesh, it is like that, only a thousand times more so. It literally lifts one out of one's seat. Next came Bessie Dudley, 'The Original Snake-Hips Girl,' who danced to the familiar 'Rockin' in Rhythm.' She has a tremendous personality, this girl, and she puts over every step of her dance with terrific rhythm.

"'The Whispering Tiger' was the next number, which of course, is our old friend 'Tiger Rag' played pianissimo throughout. Then 'Black and Tan Fantasy.'

"First encore, 'Some of These Days,' in which Fred Jenkins created a sensation.

"Second encore,'Mood Indigo.'"

After the Ellington orchestra closed at the Palladium, it played concerts around the British Isles. Its first stop was Liverpool where the Ellingtonians made 13 curtain calls and played four encores. From Liverpool they traveled to Bolton, Blackpool and

Glasgow, Scotland, where the Ellington people had a difficult time trying to understand what the Scottish people were gleefully trying to tell them about American jazz. Their message was obviously positive because all of the reviews coming out of Scotland were good. After Glasgow, they traveled to Horrogate and Birmingham and then back to London to play additional gigs.

The Ellington Orchestra was the toast at the Palladium of London in 1933 and beyond. Front row left to right: trumpets, Freddie Jenkins, "Cootie" "Williams, Art Whetsol, Duke Ellington; saxes, Otto Hardwick, Harry Carney, Johnny Hodges and Barney Bigard; Second row: trombones, Joe Nanton, Juan Tizol, and Lawrence Brown. Banjo, Fred Guy; drums, Sonny Greer; bass, Wellman Braud. It is interesting to note that in keeping with his superstition Duke had 13 members in his orchestra.

Ellington's fees were the highest ever paid in Britain to American entertainers. He was deserving of the hefty checks because his band generated the largest gross proceeds and scored successes that no Americans had paralleled. He packed the Trocadero Theater with 4,000 seated patrons and an additional 1,000 who paid to stand. It was reported that more than 100,000 listened or danced to Ellington's music prior to his leaving for Paris.

When Duke Ellington and his entourage arrived in Paris on July 27,1933, their presence almost created a riot of joy among the hundreds of Brunswick Record fans who greeted them at the train station. Duke was scheduled to perform three concerts in Paris at the huge Salle Pleyel.

According to Edgar A. Wiggins, the Chicago Defender's Paris reporter, the scene at Salle Pleyel was "one musical happiness unlike anything ever witnessed within those four walls." Wiggins further noted that the three concerts were sensationally successful. As a matter of fact, the band immortalized itself as the "Aristocrat of All Jazz Orchestras."

The Ellingtonians sailed from France on Thursday, August 3,1933, on the S.S. Majestic, leaving a never-to-be-forgotten impression. A large crowd of friends and admirers were at the Gare St. Lazaire bidding Duke and all his people bon voyage.

Weeks later, London and Paris were clamoring for Duke Ellington's return but the baggage men at Pier 59, on the North River in New York City, hoped they would never go abroad again because their baggage weighed 7,161 pounds. It took more than two hours to unload and weigh it. The baritone sax case alone weighed 200 pounds and just one of the band's music trunks weighed 350 pounds.

Although Ellington carried 1,000 pounds of music in his trunks, the English musician and music critic noted at the June 25,1933, concert in the Palladium, the orchestra played 28 numbers, all of them Ellington arrangements and 21 of them were Duke's compositions. The Englishmen were truly amazed that the orchestra used no music or music stands for a performance that lasted almost an hour. The secret was that the band had memorized most of the music in the Ellington song book.

Sonny Greer was an Ellington original in that he was Duke's drummer from 1920 to 1951. He left Duke in 1951 to join the Johnny Hodges small band.

Johnny Hodges was with Duke from May, 1928, until he formed his own small band in 1951. He rejoined Ellington in August, 1955.

Charles Melvin "Cootie" Williams joined Ellington in 1929 and remained until 1940 when he joined Benny Goodman. Later he formed his own band but returned to Duke in the fall of 1962 and remained until Duke died in 1974.

8 - THE 1930's WERE THE BEST AND WORST OF TIMES FOR DUKE

Following its British and European tour, the Ellington Orchestra became the most celebrated group of American musicians in the Western world. They were adopted by an international jazz cult without geographical or musical boundaries. Adulation of Duke was proper and fitting because the Ellington Orchestra had no peers.

The instinct to imitate Ellington's style was very strong among both American and European music makers during his lifetime and beyond.

The Duke's music, like all other arrangements, possessed four basic elements: melody, harmony, rhythm and style. "Style" is as individual as a fingerprint. Ellington's style was formulated by the mix of musicians he selected and his unorthodox method of orchestrating to fit their individual talents. Some of his greatest stars including Johnny Hodges, "Cootie" Williams, Lawrence Brown and Sonny Greer did not to excel on their respective instruments outside of the Ellington milieu.

Irving Mills recognized that Duke Ellington was riding the crest of an unprecedented popularity wave when the band returned from the Old World. Thus he decided that he would send Ellington South where there was a great demand to see those colored boys who had musically captured the hearts of Europe.

Ellington had taken a "Hell no, I won't go" posture with Irving Mills on several occasions when he was approached about touring in Dixie, the land of cotton, riverboats and tobacco. Duke was very sensitive about the inhumane conditions under which Negroes were generally forced to live and travel, irrespective of their social or economic accomplishments.

Irving Mills was prepared to counter Duke's objections about the South with a princely proposition that the band play in a chain of vaudeville houses owned by the Interstate Circuit located in Texas. Perks that goosed Duke into moving off center and accepting an offer to go below the Mason-Dixon Line were a handsome increase in salary, plus a promise from Mills that in early 1934 he would charter a home on wheels for Duke and his band. The house on rails would include two luxury Pullman sleeping cars plus a 70-foot baggage car for instruments, sound and lighting equipment as well as individual members' H&M trunks in which to keep their uniforms, street clothes and shoes.

The Southern tour on the Interstate Circuit began in Dallas on September 3,1933, in a furnace-like, stifling climate. The band played four shows a day in the air conditioned Majestic Theater and then played for dances two nights during the week after the theater gig, one on Monday night for the whites and on Thursday night for the Negroes. The boys in the orchestra blew up a "red hot and blue" funky storm at each performance. They grossed $22,000 that first week and broke the theater's all-time attendance record.

The Dallas News music critic called Ellington an "African Stravinsky," saying the "color line" between jazz and classical music was erased by five Ellington compositions, "Ring Dem Bells," "Sophisticated Lady," "It Don't Mean A Thing," "Black And Tan Fantasy," and "Mood Indigo." On the other hand, the writer was deftly silent on the color line between the races.

After the Majestic Theater gig, the Ellingtonians traveled across Texas and Oklahoma, then east to New Orleans, Birmingham, Atlanta and Memphis. Jim Crow hovered like a buzzard over every performance during the Dixie tour. In the theater the Negroes' permanent seats were usually located in the "peanut gallery," which had to be reached by climbing fire escapes on the outside of the building. The police, like an army of occupation, were always near to see that Negroes did not violate the system.

In February, 1934, Mills fulfilled his promise of getting the Ellington Orchestra its own private Pullman sleepers and a baggage car. Frequently, band members also had their own dining car and in its absence they prepared their own meals on hotplates. This new travel arrangement eliminated some frustrating and distasteful experiences of being both humiliated and rejected in search of places to eat and sleep.

The spaciousness of the Pullman coaches also eliminated the need for any of the orchestra members having to sleep in upper berths. Duke was very pleased with his new traveling arrangements. He frequently reminded those who needed to know that he traveled in the same style as Franklin Delano Roosevelt, the President of the United States.

A question frequently raised by whites and blacks: How does one write and play beautiful music when one's very soul is squashed, stomped and pulverized into the sidewalks by racism? Duke Ellington answered the query this way: "You have to try not to think about it. If you do you will knock yourself out. There are times when my cheery calm is shaken and my dressing room is more like a prison cell than a friendly saloon."

A few months after the Texas tour, the Ellington band traveled to St. Louis to play the Fox Theater. As the train pulled into Union Station, Duke's two white employees, Jack Boyd, the road manager, and Juan Tizol, the white Puerto Rican trombone player and the only white man in the band, immediately got a taxi and went to one of the town's first-class hotels. (Duke had a white man in his band seven years before Benny Goodman hired Teddy Wilson, a great Negro piano player, for a trio that included Gene Krupa on drums and Goodman on clarinet.)

Duke recalled the St.Louis stop: "I and the other members of the

Left to right: Joseph "Tricky Sam" Nanton, Juan Tizol, and Lawrence Brown.

band got taxis an hour and a half later, after considerable pleading and begging, since most white Southern drivers did not want Negroes as passengers, and if they did, they would take you to a shanty hotel in the Negro section of town.

"The next day when we went out to lunch, after our first performance, we could not find a restaurant near the Fox Theater that would serve us. We did not have time to go over to the 'Greasy Spoon' in the Black Belt" and get back before we were due on stage again.

"We returned to the theater and arranged for a white man to go out and buy sandwiches at the corner drugstore.

"When the proprietor of the store, making inquiries, found out that the sandwiches were for a Negro band, he refused to fill the order.

"A half hour later the men returned to the bandstand hungry and mad. As the curtain started to rise, the white audience gave us a burst of applause, followed by cheers, whistles and stomping feet.

"Once the curtain was up, the dejection on the faces of the men in the orchestra vanished as quickly as one can click an electrical switch. The dour look on their faces turned to one of joy. Everything was flash and brightness until the curtain came down. The joyful faces vanished and my beautiful people turned into a group of angry, hungry Negroes arguing among themselves about their right to eat.

"The manager of the Fox Theater was called and he admitted that if the band was to work it should be allowed to eat. He arranged for food to be sent in. After finishing the meal, Boyd, my white road manager, went across the street to a saloon overlooking the stage door. A white woman sitting next to him at the bar saw one of the men in our band come out of the stage door and get into a taxi. She turned to Boyd and said:

"Did you see that"'

"See what?" Boyd said.

"See that Nigra get in that cab?"

"Well, he is a pretty nice fellow. He's a member of the Ellington Band. Some people think he is a great artist."

"A very great artist?" she repeated. "Well, I don't know what you think, but I always say that the worst white man is better than the best Nigra."

Duke frequently said that he tried to forget unpleasant experiences. He further stated that if he did not quite succeed in forgetting some of the saddest stories ever told, he pretended that he did.

Duke's world crumbled on his head when on May 27,1935, he lost his mother who had been his life. All of his creative efforts begged her approval. Nobody else's opinion about his work meant more to him than what she thought. His whole world had been built around pleasing his mother. When she died, his creativity went into suspension. His ambition hit rock bottom.

When Duke's mother was on her death bed in a sanitarium in

An hour before show times at the Regal. Left, Jack Boyd, Ellington road manager; right at the vibes , Joseph "Tricky Sam" Nanton. Background center between Nanton and Boyd is Harry Carney, baritone sax player.

Detroit in April, 1935, he wrote "In a Sentimental Mood," one of the most yearning, haunting melodies ever to drip from the Ellington pen.

In the summer of 1935 he wrote "Reminiscing in Tempo," a creative reflection on his beloved mother's life and her passing. He said the manuscript he used was stained with tears.

The tear drops on that paper never dried during his lifetime.

Jack Johnson, the first Black World Heavyweight Champion.

Jesse Owens established himself as the world's fastest human at the 1936 Olympics held in Berlin, Germany .

Kenneth Blewett, manager of the Regal Theater, introduces Joe Louis, the second Negro World Heavyweight Champion, to Duke Ellington

9 - ELLINGTON: A SYMBOL OF LIBERATION

D uke Ellington was more than a great musician, he was a hero in the Negro communities across the nation. People of color bathed in his success. His music and his presence brought hopes of liberation from racial oppression to many who seldom saw any sunshine in their lives. Duke was a winner in a closed society that had a record of not having very many colored escapees. Prior to Ellington, Jack Johnson, the first Negro heavyweight champion, and Marcus Garvey, an international civil rights leader, were two of the most visible symbols of Negro liberation.

In the summer of 1936, Jesse Owens became another symbol when he established himself as the world's fastest human and one of the greatest track athletes in history at the Olympics held that year in Berlin, Germany. Hope was offered every Negro by those sepia colored brothers and sisters who broke barriers like Marian Anderson and William Grant Still in music; George Washington Carver and Dr. Percy Julian in science; Madam C. J. Walker and Anthony Overton in business, as well as others in track, baseball, basketball, football, and other endeavors.

Duke Ellington's attitude toward life and music began to show slight signs of optimism in 1936 as he slowly came out from under an umbrella of depression following his mother's death in May 1935. The uplift in his spirit was manifested in four of the seven songs that he wrote in 1936: "Oh Babe, Maybe Someday," "Trumpet In Spades," "Echoes of Harlem," and "Caravan."

Ellington got an opportunity to showcase his new material when his band followed the Benny Goodman Orchestra into the Urban Room of Chicago's Congress Hotel on May 8,1936. His gig was for only four weeks, whereas Goodman had played in the room for 28 consecutive weeks.The month's engagement for Duke included air time three times a night on a local radio station and twice weekly on the NBC National Network. The national radio exposure followed a two-year absence from the airwaves for Duke Ellington during a period when nightly national hookup carried a multitude of white swing bands, including Glenn Miller, Artie Shaw, Jack

Teagarden, Tommy Dorsey, Jimmy Dorsey, Glen Gray, Bob Crosby, Red Norvo and Benny Goodman. Negro newspapers such as the Chicago Defender, Pittsburgh Courier and the New York Amsterdam News had been very vocal in accusing the radio networks of discriminating against the Ellingtonians.

The 1935 Goodman Orchestra. Standing second from right is Benny Goodman

While Duke Ellington was playing at the Congress Hotel, he slept at the Ritz Hotel on the southeast corner of South Parkway and Oakland Boulevard in the heart of the "Black Belt" and next door to the Grand Terrace where the Earl Hines Orchestra played nightly. Negroes were not accepted as guests at any of Chicago's downtown hotels. As a matter of fact, that discriminatory policy remained in force until the mid-50's. Case in point: when Teddy Wilson, the very talented pianist, officially joined the Goodman Trio in April of 1936 at the Congress Hotel, he was stopped at the front entrance by the doorman when he attempted to enter the building and directed to take the freight elevator at the rear of the hotel. Wilson was allowed to enter the front door after John Hammond, a Vanderbilt heir, jazz impresario, and Benny

Goodman's brother-in-law had a civil rights session with the hotel management.

During Ellington's engagement at the Congress Hotel he met Helen Oakley, a highly talented 19-year-old white female jazz writer for Downbeat Magazine and the Chicago Herald-Examiner. She wrote several articles about the band for both the Downbeat and the Examiner. Duke was so impressed with her writing and public relation skills he asked Irving Mills to latch onto her before she got away. Mills hired Oakley and she moved to New York City in the summer of 1936 to be a part of Irving Mills's staff.

Helen Oakley has been credited with persuading Irving Mills to record small groups within the Ellington Orchestra. In December, 1936, she began producing recording sessions for the small Ellington groups on Mills's Variety label. Leadership of the small band within the band rotated among Johnny Hodges, Barney Bigard, "Cootie" Williams and Rex Stewart. Ellington played the piano on all recording dates because he was in deep financial debt as a result of his lavish lifestyle and his mother's astronomically high medical and hospital bills.

In January and February, 1937, the Ellingtonians completed a six-week tour on the West Coast before returning east to open at the Cotton Club on March 15. Following the 1935 Harlem race riot, the Cotton Club had moved to 48th Street between Broadway and Seventh Avenue in midtown Manhattan.

The Cotton Club moved from 145th and Lenox Avenue in Harlem to midtown Manhattan on 48th Street between 7th and Broadway.

The Duke Ellington aggregation arrived in the Windy City enroute to New York on March 1 at 8:50 a.m. on the modern two-tone gray, silver strip Santa Fe Chief. They quickly transferred by cab to the Pennsylvania station to catch the Manhattan Limited which pulled out of Chicago exactly two hours later.

The crack, silver strip Santa Fe Chief was within one hour of reaching Chicago when this picture was taken.

During the brief layover, Barney Bigard, masterful New Orleans-style clarinet player, was interviewed by the Chicago Defender, which quoted him as saying the band had enjoyed a remarkable success in California and was looking forward to opening in the New Cotton Club Revue in New York with such talented performers as Ethel Waters, the Pekin Boys and a quintet of "streamlined" Chicago bronze beauties specially picked for the new production. The Duke Ellington Orchestra was replacing the famous Cab Calloway Orchestra at the internationally famous Broadway nite club.

On April 29,1937, Duke Ellington celebrated his 38th birthday at the Cotton Club, where he was broadcasting four times weekly over the Mutual Network. Ellington was also observing his 10th year as a brand-name band leader and one of America's foremost composers. Four musicians who played in Duke's five-piece band at the Kentucky Club a decade earlier were known as the originals in an orchestra that had grown to 15 members. The original five, including the Duke, were Arthur Whetsol, trumpet; Sonny Greer, drums; Otto Hardwick, saxophone, and Fred Guy, banjo and guitar.

By 1937 Duke Ellington had written more than 100 songs, many of them played by his orchestra but never reduced to manuscript. This practice was not uncommon for the Duke because some of his tunes, now recognized as classics, were played at dances and in theaters around the country for months before being put on paper.

Barney Bigard joined Duke in December, 1927, and left in the summer of 1942. He joined Louis Armstrong in August, 1947, and stayed until the summer of 1952.

It was projected in the early 1930's by music critics and some of Duke Ellington's more astute fellow piano players that his capacity for melodic invention had scarcely been tapped. One really did not have to be a Harvard trained Dr. W. E. B. DuBois to make such a prediction because in 1937 Ellington had 15 new songs copyrighted and 31 more copyrighted in 1938. Included in those 46 works were some of Ellington's most memorable compositions such as "Caravan," "I've Got To Be A Rug Cutter," "Black Butterfly," "Pyramid," "Lost in Meditation," "Empty Ballroom Blues," "Jeep's Blues," "I Let A Song Go Out Of My Heart," "Prelude To A Kiss," "Swingtime In Honolulu," "Braggin' In Brass" and "Carnival In Caroline".

Duke, like all champions, had to rest between rounds. Although he was musically productive in 1937 and 1938, he was laboring under knockout personal problems. Duke's father, James Edward Ellington, died on October 28, 1937, at Columbia Presbyterian Hospital in New York City. The senior Ellington's death was hastened by drinking problems that had developed over a period of years. J. E., as he was affectionately known, was Duke's mentor, surrogate brother and father who traveled regularly with his son during his last years. The loss of his father and mother at early ages, within a two-year span, were crosses almost too heavy for the Duke to bear.

The Duke Ellington Primer

Duke replaced the famous Cab Calloway Orchestra at the Cotton Club in 1937.

Duke was physically knocked down and forced to undergo a hernia operation on August 15,1938. While confined to bed for three weeks, he wrote this statement for the Negro Actors Magazine:

"The skyline from my windows in the Wickersham Hospital is an inspiring sight. I have spent three weeks here, not too ill to be thrilled daily by a view of these skyscrapers, and with plenty of time for ample meditation.

"It is natural perhaps, that I should think of many subjects, some serious, some fanciful. I spent some time comparing the marvelous skyline to our race, likening Chrysler Tower, the Empire State Building and other lofty structures to the lives of Bert Williams, the comic's comic; Florence Mills, the famous Broadway singer and dancer, and other immortals of the entertainment field.

"I mused over the qualities which these stars possessed that enabled them to tower as far above their fellow artist as do these buildings above the skyline.

"And it seemed to me, from where I was lying, that in addition to their great talent, the qualities which have made really great stars are those of simplicity, sincerity and a rigid adherence to the traditions of our own people.

"We are children of the sun and our race has a definite tradition of beauty and glory and vitality that is rich and powerful as the sun itself. These traditions are ours to express, and will enrich our careers in proportion to the sincerity and faithfulness with which we interpret them."

In addition to writing poetically about his people, Duke walked picket lines with Rev. Adam Clayton Powell, Jr., in protest of the discriminatory hiring policies of Consolidated Edison Light Company. Ellington also musically expressed the plight of the Negro through his work in "Jump For Joy" and "Black, Brown and Beige."

In 1938, the Pittsburgh Courier criticized Duke because none of the lyrics to his songs had been written by Negroes during the period he was under the Irving Mills banner. That criticism was mooted when Ellington severed his relationship with Mills in 1939 for reasons that he never expressed publicly. However according to Marian "Birdie-May" Logan, wife of Ellington's physician Arthur C. Logan, one day Duke walked into Mills's office and asked to see the books. He perused them and left without saying a word. Marian said that Duke discovered that Mills had purchased a coffin for his mother's burial for a sum less than the $5,000 that Ellington had instructed Mills to spend. Mills doubtless did not understand the depth of love Duke had for his mother, expressed by Duke when he purchased $2,000 worth of flowers for his mother's funeral. The dollar amount for flowers is significant when you consider that the monthly wage for a WPA worker with a family in 1935 was only $55. Duke had spent approximately four years of a worker's wage on flowers for his mother's funeral. Knowing how Duke felt about his mother, one could safely conclude that Mills's failure to fulfill Ellington's wishes about her coffin was the treacherous cut that severed the long-standing business relationship between the two men.

Duke took a 15-minute intermission between parting with Irving Mills and signing up with the William Morris office as his new management agency. For Ellington, it was a brand new day.

10 - ELLINGTON AND STRAYHORN, THE COMPATIBLE GENIUSES

During the first four decades of the 20th century the presence of an upright piano in the living room indicated that a family had reached a social and economic status that was at least two notches above the underclass. Both Duke Ellington and Billy Strayhorn lived in homes that had pianos. Thus, in the eyes of most Negroes, they were considered members of a privileged class.

As pre-teenagers, Duke looked at the piano with gloom whereas Billy looked at it with glee. The giant-sized musical instrument occupied a major share of the parlor wall, weighed approximately 500 pounds and measured 4.7 feet in height and 5 feet in width. The guts of the piano were usually encased in a reddish-brown wood finish with a long 4.5 feet mouth running across the center of its face, exposing 88 protruding ebony-and-ivory caped teeth.

Ellington did not get turned on to piano until he discovered that it was a honey trap for catching pretty girls. Whereas Billy Strayhorn's sister, Lillian Dicks, remembers her teenage brother playing piano incessantly in their small four-room house in Homewood, a Negro section of Pittsburgh. "I guess I got used to it, like living near the railroad," she recalls.

The Pittsburgh metropolis was known as the "Smokey City" because smoke and smog from the steel mills hung over it as an impenetrable curtain. On some days, at high noon, the smoke and smog blanketed the sun like a total eclipse.

Mrs. Dicks also remembers Strayhorn's sense of style. "My brother did not walk around the house in his pants because they would lose their crease and also get wrinkled. So my earliest recollections were of him in his boxer shorts sitting and playing the piano."

The Strayhorn's home, which is now a vacant lot, stood on the corner at Cassina Way and Zenith Way behind a still-standing red brick church.

His sister vividly recollects, "The minister came over to our home and requested that Billy not play the piano in such a vigorous manner during the Sunday morning service because he was

Duke Ellington admired pretty women and they in turn admired him. When he said: "I love you madly," he was serious.

distracting the congregation."

During his early teens, Strayhorn occupied himself with lessons in European classical piano, music theory, composition, and boys at the Westinghouse High School and the Musical Institute. He studied piano with Jane Patton Alexander, and he played piano in the school orchestra under Carl McVickers, one of Pittsburgh's most celebrated music teachers.

Strayhorn studied Bach, Beethoven and Brahms. He loved Ravel and Rachmaninoff. When he played Gershwin he was "stepping down," according to Mrs. Dicks. For his graduation recital, Billy performed Grieg's "Piano Concerto" with the orchestra.

Strayhorn was not attracted to jazz music until he heard the Duke Ellington Orchestra at the Stanley Theater shortly after he graduated from high school in the spring of 1934. He instantly became addicted to Ellington's unconventional musical style after just two deep sniffs.

Between 1932 and 1938, Strayhorn worked as a soda jerk at the

Pennfield Pharmacy in Point Breeze. Drugstore customers who had heard his piano work during his high school years regularly reminded him that he should do something with his music in the tradition of other Pittsburghers such as: Earl Hines, one of America's greatest jazz piano players; Billy Eckstine, the handsome vocalist who subsequently became the pioneering leader of a be-bop band that included Charlie "Yard Bird" Parker, John "Dizzy" Gillespie, Gene Ammons, Howard McGee, Fats Navarro, Tadd Dameron, and Sarah Vaughan; Lena Horne, the beautiful Pittsburgh teenager who danced as a Cotton Club chorus girl and gained fame and fortune as a singer, movie star and civil rights activist; Mary Lou Williams, a product of the "Smokey City" became a piano player and arranger for the Andy Kirk Orchestra, as well as a writer for Benny Goodman, Tommy Dorsey, Louis Armstrong and Duke Ellington, and Maxine Sullivan, the young Pittsburgh vocalist who gave the Scottish folk song "Loch Lomond" a jazz beat that made it an American best selling recording in 1938. Pittsburgh also gave the jazz world Erroll Garner and

Duke Ellington and his Cotton Club Orchestra

Ahmad Jamal, both great creative piano players.

As a sideline Strayhorn did something with his talents by organizing a jazz trio called The Mad Hatters that played occasional social club gigs and house-rent parties in addition to broadcasting 15 minutes daily for several months from a local radio station. Strayhorn never made enough money gigging nor mustered enough courage at the age of 22 to quit his job at the drugstore and venture into the music business on a full-time basis.

A 1928 picture of Earl Hines, one of the world's great jazz piano players.

A 1944 picture of Billy Eckstine, a ballard and blues singer extraordinaire.

On December 2,1938, Strayhorn was cajoled by his good friend William Esch, the arranger for an all-girl jazz band directed by Chicagoan Ina Ray Hutton, to meet with Duke Ellington. With Esch's foot at his lower back, Strayhorn reluctantly journeyed through the Pittsburgh hills to the downtown stage door of the Stanley Theater to keep an appointment with Ellington pre-arranged by Esch. The mannerly young man, groomed in the Esquire Magazine style, was admitted backstage where he subsequently introduced himself to Mr. Ellington as the maestro hurriedly walked off the stage enroute to his dressing room.

Duke, whom the author had always found to be easy to talk to, invited Strayhorn to play some of his original works on the portable piano which he kept in his dressing room. Duke had heard about Billy's writing skills from Esch. Ellington was fascinated with the lyrics of Strayhorn's music and indicated that he would like to have Billy join the band if he could arrange to find a slot for him when he returned to New York City. Strayhorn had played two of his beautiful compositions during the interview, they were: "Lush Life" and "Something To Live For." Ellington was seriously impressed by the haunting tones and the depth of both the melody and the lyrics of "Lush Life," now considered by many musicians as the mother of all torch songs. Strayhorn's lyrics in "Lush Life" expressed the following sentiment: "A Week in Paris

A 1953 picture of Ahmad Jamal at the Pershing Hotel in Chicago.

Erroll Garner at the Blue Note in Chicago in 1958.

Will Ease the Bite of It." His lyrical voicing was both sophisticated and harmonically exciting. The lyrics were of genius quality when you consider that Strayhorn wrote the songs when he was only a 16-year-old high school student. His only knowledge of Paris came from studying French in secondary school and from reading the New Yorker magazine regularly.

Several months passed without Strayhorn hearing anything from Ellington in reference to being hired. As luck would have it, William Esch, his arranger friend, had to drive to New York City to transact some business for his boss Ina Ray Hutton. Esch suggested that Billy come along for the ride, and when they reached Newark, Strayhorn accidently discovered while drinking a milk shake and scanning a local newspaper, that Duke Ellington was playing in that city at the Adams Theater. Strayhorn made a beeline to the backstage door of the Adams Theater to see Ellington. His stomach churned double time after being permitted to stand in the wings and watch the show. When Duke came off the bandstand he sensed Strayhorn's discomfort the moment they exchanged greetings. Ellington tried to arrest Billy's nervousness with the warmth of his personality. As a matter of fact, Ellington told the young musician as they walked to his dressing room that he had called his office in New York City that morning in an effort to find his telephone number so he could invite Strayhorn to join the Duke's band.

In the very next breath, Duke handed Strayhorn several pieces of sheet music from the dressing table and instructed him to arrange them. The two songs, "Like A Ship In The Night" and "Savoy Strut," were for the Johnny Hodges small band. Hodges subsequently recorded the two arrangements in February and March of 1939.

Strayhorn was not comfortable with the assignment because he

had never written a single arrangement in his life and his only scoring experience had been limited to what he had learned at the Pittsburgh Musical Institute and what he gleaned looking over the shoulder of his friend William Esch. Billy had told Duke "straight up" that he did not know how to arrange. Ellington overrode that negative attitude with the same kind of psychology that he later employed on Clark Terry when he told Terry that he was like Buddy Bolden, New Orleans' legendary first great jazz trumpet player. Duke psyched Terry into playing big round notes like Bolden for the "The Drum Was A

Duke and Billy at the piano backstage in the dressing room.

Woman" recording date.

Billy's only explanation for the success he had in producing his two initial arrangements, which Duke found flawless, flowed from the confidence Ellington had injected in him. From 1939 forward Duke did very few arrangements for the small bands within his band. He turned almost all of that writing over to Billy Strayhorn.

Following the Newark Adams Theater gig Duke opened at the Apollo Theater on 125th Street in New York's Harlem where he had been booked for a one-week engagement to be filled just prior to the orchestra's leaving the states for another European tour in late March, 1939.

Mercer Ellington was asked by his father to take care of Billy Strayhorn until he returned from Europe. Initially Mercer assisted Strayhorn in finding a room at the 135th Street YMCA in Harlem.

Strayhorn had not been in his "Y" room an hour before he took off to pay his first all-day visit to the Ellington's Sugar Hill apartment at 409 Edgecombe. In fact, Billy spent so much time at the apartment studying the Ellington scores that Mercer decided to move Billy and all his belongings into their huge Edgecombe apartment, which sat near the top of Sugar Hill overlooking the Polo Grounds.

Other luminaries, who were tenants in the 14-story 409 Edgecombe building included Dr. W.E.B. DuBois, the Harvard scholar and author, whose apartment on the 13th-floor was known as the White House of Harlem because dignitaries from all over the world came to visit the brilliant man on his own turf; Thurgood Marshall, who later became the first Negro member of the Supreme Court during the Lyndon Johnson administration; Walter White and Roy Wilkins, top officials of the NAACP; and Josh White, the internationally renowned folk singer. When Duke returned from Europe he found that Mercer, his sister Ruth and Billy had taken on a comfortable family-like relationship.

For a brief period while Ellington was in Europe, Strayhorn

In 1939, the Ellington family lived at 409 Edgecombe, near the top of Sugar Hill, in Washington Heights. 409 was the choicest address for Negro Harlemites.

played piano in the Mercer Ellington Band. Following the Mercer gig Billy played and wrote for the Duke Ellington Orchestra for the balance of his life. However, there are some Duke snoops who suspect that Strayhorn wrote several arrangements on the side for the Charlie Barnet Orchestra.

A dispute between the Broadcast Music Inc. (BMI), an American performing rights society founded in 1940 by broadcasters in New York City, and the American Society of Composers, Authors, and

Publishers (ASCAP) founded in 1914 in New York, had been simmering before the Duke left for Europe. The two groups were sparring and talking trash in preparation for an impending lawsuit over who should control the performing fees collected by ASCAP for the members' compositions that were played on the radio.

The first punch was thrown by the BMI radio people who banned  from the airwaves all music written by ASCAP members. In addition to legal action taken by ASCAP, Duke personally reacted to the attack on his compositions by bringing his young gladiators, namely his son Mercer and Strayhorn, into the fray. Both young men were excellent writers, but not members of ASCAP.

The band had an engagement early in January, 1941, at the Casa Manana in Los Angeles, and a nightly broadcast. The Ellington "Young Lions" had to create an instant new library.

A 1914 picture of Dr. W.E.B. DuBois Strayhorn and Mercer got busy arranging and writing so they could take advantage of the air time.

During the radio ban against ASCAP members, Strayhorn composed "Day Dream" and "Passion Flower" for the Johnny Hodges band and "Take The 'A' Train," which was first recorded on January 15,1941. It subsequently became the Ellington theme song. Some of the other songs he wrote included "After All," "Chelsea Bridge," "I Don't Mind," "Johnny Came Later," "Raincheck," "Clementine" and a number of other arrangements for the Ellington orchestra. Meanwhile Mercer Ellington wrote such memorable works as: "Moon Mist," "Blue Serge," "John Hardy's Wife" and "Things Ain't What They Used To Be," which became a big hit during the World War II years and is still a standard today.

The battle between ASCAP and BMI provided both a springboard and opportunity for Billy Strayhorn to exercise his writing and arranging skills. Ellington had initially thought of Strayhorn as a lyricist because of the talent he displayed in writing the lyrics for

"Lush Life." Duke's limiting fence around Billy's talents was trashed because between 1940 and 1941, Strayhorn proved that he had musical abilities that went far beyond matching words to music. His elevation in the Ellington operation was accomplished without his ever displaying any signs of artistic arrogance. Billy, like his boss, was an all-around gifted musician; the two men were psychologically and musically in tune with each other. Duke and other members of the band alternately called Billy "Strays" and "Swee' Pea." The nickname Swee' Pea was given him by Lena

Left to right: Melvin James "Sy" Oliver, the arranger for the famous Jimmie Lunceford Orchestra and later for the Tommy Dorsey Band, Duke Ellington and Billy Strayhorn.

Horne, for whom he also did arranging.

Duke frequently described "Strays" as the most unselfish, the most patient, and the most imperturbable person he had ever known. Musically, no individual was closer to Duke Ellington than Billy Strayhorn. "Stray's" arrangements and writings for the orchestra were so similar to Ellington's that lifetime members of the band were frequently baffled trying to figure out where Duke stopped and Strayhorn began. Strayhorn composed about 200 works alone or in collaboration with Ellington during their 28-year partnership. In addition, he arranged hundreds of songs for

Ellington's big and small orchestras.

Billy Strayhorn died of cancer of the esophagus at age 51 on May 31, 1967, in New York City.

Moments before the funeral was scheduled to begin on June 5, 1967, at 10:30 a.m. in the 19th century St. Peter's Lutheran Church, 54th Street and Lexington Avenue, Duke Ellington entered the church and took a seat in the front pew, center aisle.

The service began with the gentle notes of "Blues for Strayhorn" drifting from choir loft. Randy Weston had written the song for Billy two years earlier. When his trio finished playing the song, Randy said: "I never thought I'd end up playing it at his funeral. It

Left to right: Art Blakey, Johnny Griffin, Chicago's Mayor Harold Washington, Randy Weston, Dempsey Travis . Chicago Kool Jazz Festival 1984

was difficult."

The 350 mourners for the most part remained composed however. They were overwhelmed when Ray Nance, violinist, and the Billy Taylor Trio opened a collection of Strayhorn compositions with a dirgelike version of "Take the 'A' Train."

Jackie Robinson, the former baseball star, said, "I don't think there was a dry eye in the church when they finished playing 'A' Train."

Lena Horne, Benny Goodman, Milt Jackson, Otto Preminger, the movie producer, and John Hammond were among those at Strayhorn's services.

The following eulogy for "Sweetpea" was written by Duke Ellington:

"Poor little 'Sweetpea,' Billy Strayhorn, William Thomas Strayhorn, the biggest human being who ever lived, a man with the greatest courage, the most majestic artistic stature, a highly skilled musician whose impeccable taste commanded the respect of all musicians and the admiration of all listeners.

"His audience at home and abroad marveled at the great grandeur of his talent and the mantle of tonal supremacy that he wore only with grace. He was a beautiful human being, adored by a wide range of friends, rich, poor, famous, and unknown. Great artists pay homage to Billy Strayhorn's God-given ability and mastery of his craft.

"Because he had a rare sensitivity and applied himself to his gifts, Billy Strayhorn successfully married melody, words, and harmony, equating the fitting with happiness. His greatest virtue, I think, was his honesty, not only to others but to himself. His listening-hearing self was totally intolerant of his writing-playing self when or if any compromise was expected, or considered expedient.

"He spoke English perfectly and French very well, but condescension did not enter into his mind. He demanded freedom of expression and lived in what we consider the most important and moral of freedoms: freedom from hate, unconditionally; freedom from all self-pity (even through-out all the pain and bad news); freedom from fear of possibly doing something that might help another more than it might help himself; and freedom from the kind of pride that could make a man feel he was better than his brother or his neighbor.

"His patience was incomparable and unlimited. He had no aspirations to enter into any kind of competition, yet the legacy he leaves, his oeuvre, will never be less than the ultimate on the highest plateau of culture (whether by comparison or not).

"God bless Billy Strayhorn."

The Parkway Ballroom was remodeled in 1985 and converted into the executive offices of the Chicago Metropolitan Mutual Assurance Company.

Jimmy Blanton signed on with the Duke Ellington Orchestra in the autumn of 1939. He died at age 24 of Tuberculosis on July 30, 1942 in Los Angeles, Ca.

Ben Webster joined Ellington for the third time in January, 1940, left Duke in 1943 to lead his own small band on 52nd Street. He rejoined Duke for the fourth time in November, 1948. He died in Amsterdam, Holland, on September 20,1973.

11 - DUKE WATCHING IN CHICAGO DURING THE 1940'S

I closed my 1940 music diary with notes about the Duke Ellington Orchestra filling the new and beautiful, Negro-owned Parkway Ballroom, 4457 South Parkway, with his musical magic on Friday, December 6. Several musician friends and I stood a few inches from the center of the bandstand, rocking in rhythm for three and a half solid hours of melodic joy. We did not move even when the band took several 15-minute intermissions, for fear of losing our space.

Being within arm's reach of the Duke Ellington Orchestra was space worth fighting for. Duke had expanded the band and added Jimmy Blanton on bass in the fall of 1939 and Ben "The Brute" Webster on tenor sax in January, 1940. During one of his bar-hopping excursions, Billy Strayhorn discovered Blanton working in an after-hours joint in St. Louis. The Ellington band was in the Missouri town fulfilling a three-week engagement at the beautiful Club Caprice in the Hotel Coronado.

In March, 1935, Billy Taylor joined the Ellington Orchestra as one of its bass players, sharing bass playing duties with Wellman Braud and later with Hayes Alvis. He was Ellington's sole bass player when Blanton came aboard.

Jimmy Blanton had a tone and beat that created a propelling pulsation that synchronized the rhythm section and rhythmically pushed the entire orchestra to another level of swing. His instrumental technique was unlike any other jazz bass player on the planet. In January, 1940, a little less than three months after Blanton joined the band, Billy Taylor quit in the middle of a dance set at the Southland Cafe in Boston. As he walked off the bandstand he said, "I am not going to let no young bass player embarrass me in public."

Webster's presence, like Blanton's, gave the orchestra another dimension, increasing the sax section for the first time to five men. Other members of the section were Barney Bigard, Johnny Hodges, Toby Hardwick and Harry Carney. Ben Webster brought a cohesiveness and a Kansas City swing style to a sax section that was long overdue in light of what was happening in the reed sections of the Count Basie, Jimmie Lunceford, Benny Goodman, Woody Herman, Glenn Miller and the Andy Kirk Orchestras.

Billy Taylor, at right, quit the Ellington Orchestra three months after Blanton came abroad.

Ben Webster had a style that was both harsh and tender, depending on the tune. For example, he figuratively kissed you when he played "All Too Soon." On the other hand, he made your backbone twitch and your toes itch when he blew "Cotton Tail."

Everybody in the Parkway Ballroom that December night stopped dancing and stood still for several spellbound moments when the copper-colored, handsome and slender, 22-year-old Jimmy Blanton soloed. Strong pulsations from the strings of his bass fiddle sent tremors through your soul as he plucked melodic solos on "Jack The Bear" and "Sepia Panorama." The young musician radically increased the scope of the four-string bass for living bass players and those yet unborn. No electronic devices were needed in a ballroom or theater to hear Blanton because he played from scratch with his God-given talent, his imagination, his bow and his bare finger tips.

Notes in my diary indicate that I opened my musical leap year one month and a day late on Friday, February 2,1940, without the slightest notion that the year would be one of Duke's most productive song writing years. He recorded 29 of his compositions which made this a very fruitful year.

My first entries for the year were observations of the Duke Ellington Orchestra and Show opening at the State-Lake Theater in Chicago's Loop.

State-Lake Theater, Chicago, Illinois 1942

The morning of February 2 was extremely cold. The Chicago "Hawk" was whirling around every corner like a ballerina. Several of my musical buddies and I almost turned into ice cubes as we waited in line for the theater to open. The only thing warm about me were my thoughts of how I would be made warmer than toast by Ellington's sizzling music.

The early morning theater line was more than a block long snaking north on State Street a quarter of a block and around the corner westward for one block along Lake Street to Dearborn. Duke's drawing power was then without equal in Chicago. He was competing with Dorothy Lamour, the co-star in many of the Bing Crosby-Bob Hope road pictures and a former Marshall Field's elevator girl, who was one of the most popular Hollywood stars of the period. She was appearing in person directly across the street from the State-Lake at the Chicago Theater. A half block south on Randolph Street, the Oriental Theater was showing "Gone With The Wind," a brand new movie that was the talk of the nation and has become a film classic.

The Chicago Theater which opened in 1923 on the north end of State Street in the Loop, then known as the "great street."

Hoagy Carmichael, one of American's great songwriters. His songs include: "Stardust," "Rocking Chair," "Lazy River" and "Georgia On My Mind."

The Ellington stage show alone more than compensated for the below- zero temperature and very high wind. Vocal renditions by Ivie Anderson and Herb Jeffries generated some jazz heat for which they each received a number of encore calls after each performance. In the 1930's and 40's, theater performers did multiples of four to five stage shows a day.

Herb Jeffries, new with the Ellington band, added another theatrical dimension to the bill. Duke knew the Jeffries family in Detroit and whenever the band came there to play at the Paradise Theater or the Graystone Ballroom, Jeffries would show up with his hip talk doing his vocal impersonations of Bing Crosby for anyone who would listen.

Earl Hines invited Herb to come up on the bandstand and sing Mitchell Parish and Hoagy Carmichael's "Stardust" in a Bing Crosbyish high-voice fashion one night when the band was playing at the East-Wood Gardens in Detroit. He hired him on the spot because he thought the kid was good. The 6' 2", blue-eyed mulatto was also handsome enough for Hines to think he would make an excellent matinee idol. While with Hines, Jeffries was discovered by a movie producer who enticed him to leave the Hines Orchestra and make movies. Herb made a series of sepia western cowboy movies and became known in a relatively short period of time across America as the "Singing Bronze Buckeroo."

Bill Bailey, one of the smoother tap dancers. Otto Hardwick and Juan Tizol are seen in the background.

Duke had not been in the market for a male singer. The only ones he had used were members of the band, including Cootie Williams, Ray Nance and Sonny Greer, who doubled on instruments and sang. However, Herb Jeffries was so eager to work with the Duke that he agreed to travel with the band for expenses and a little walking-around money. Billy Strayhorn arranged Edmond Anderson and Ted Grouya's new song "Flamingo" for Herb, with the understanding that he would have to lower his voice. It became a big hit in 1940 and also part of music history.

In addition to Ivie Anderson and Herb Jeffries, the Ellington's star-studded review included the popular dancing team of Danny and Edith, plus Bill Bailey, the brother of singer Pearl Bailey. Bill was reputed to be the second Bill "Bojangles" Robinson because he could lay those iron taps down, on wood or concrete, in the style of Bojangles. An extra, extra attraction on the bill: The two Zephyrs, a comic pantomime dance team.

Following the State-Lake's movie was the main event: Duke Ellington and his Orchestra, plus the entertainers. Several min-

Rex Stewart joined Ellington in December, 1934, and stayed, except for short breaks, until April, 1943. He organized his own band and rejoined Duke in October, 1943, staying until December, 1945. Stewart died in Los Angeles on September 7, 1947

utes after the movie ended, the curtain was lifted to reveal a dark stage, suddenly illuminated with an amber spotlight focused on Duke Ellington, dressed to kill, standing at a white elevated piano playing a medley of some of his most popular works. Duke's appearance evoked thunderous applause. As the band rocked softly, Ellington, with his customary flair, introduced each member of the band. Each musician stood in turn as his name was called to bathe briefly in the spotlight.

After introductions, the stage lights were turned up and Ellington led the orchestra from the piano into his version of Rachmaninoff's "Preclude in C Sharp Minor." Singing and dancing acts followed the opening number with the band playing accompanimental music interspersed with Ellington compositions such as "Please Forgive Me," featuring soloist Lawrence Brown on trombone and "Cootie" Williams on trumpet; "Gal From Joe's," featuring Johnny Hodges on alto saxophone; "Caravan," featuring Juan Tizol on valve trombone; "Jeep Is Jumpin'" and "Jeep's Blues," featuring Johnny "Wimpy" Hodges; "I'm Checking Out - Goom Bye," featuring trumpet soloist "Cootie" Williams, Joe "Tricky Sam" Nanton on slide trombone, and vocalist Ivie Anderson; "Me And You," solo by Ivie Anderson; "Concerto For Cootie," featuring "Cootie" Williams; an unforgettable "Boy Meets Horn," a trumpet solo by Rex Stewart. The house was tranquilized by "Sophisticated Lady," featuring Lawrence Brown on slide trombone, Harry Carney on baritone saxophone, Johnny Hodges on alto saxophone and Duke Ellington at piano.

On Friday, February 9, Duke carried the same stage show into the Regal Theater on the South Side of Chicago where the featured film was "Barricade" starring Warner Baxter and Alice Faye.

Lighting fixtures and stage settings were the property of the band and reportedly cost $20,000, enough in 1933 to buy four six-

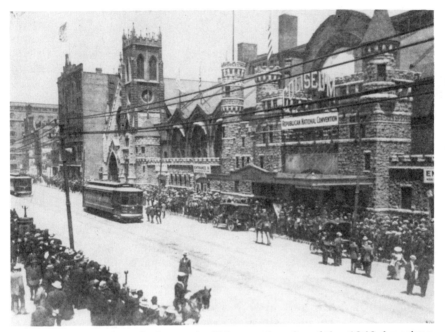

A 1916 picture of the Coliseum in Chicago, the site of the 1940 American Negro Exposition.

flat buildings in good condition. These expensive fixtures were carried in a special baggage car attached to the two Pullman cars that transported the band.

After completing two weeks of successful engagements at the State-Lake and the Regal Theaters, Duke Ellington and his famous orchestra hit the road playing dance dates at Wayne State University in Detroit, and then on to Muskegon, Michigan, February 17; Grand Rapids, February 18 to 20; Ann Arbor, February 23 and 24; Lansing, February 25 to 28; South Bend, Indiana, February 29; and ended the tour in Saginaw, Michigan, on March 3, 4 and 5.

The Duke Ellington aggregation returned to Chicago on August 26,1940, to perform at the American Negro Exposition, held at the Coliseum located at 14th Street and Wabash Avenues. The

Zinky Cohn, renowned pianist who accompanied Marva Louis, Ethel Waters, Eddie "the Black Angel of the Violin," South , Stuff Smith and Jimmy Noone, just to mention a few.

Exposition, which ran from July 4 to September 2, was to celebrate nationwide the 75th anniversary of Negro emancipation.

August 26 was Duke Ellington Day at the Exposition. I went with Zinky Cohn, who was accompanist for vocalist Ethel "Stormy Weather" Waters, 1934, and pianist for Eddie "Dark Angel of the Violin" South Orchestra, 1936; Jimmy "Sweet Lorraine" Noone, Benny Goodman's mentor, 1929-31; and Erskine Tate, Louis Armstrong's former band leader, 1932. Cohn, the business manager for the Musician Union Local 208, and I witnessed the Ellington orchestra in its rarest form. Duke's dance-concert included 42 numbers, beginning with his theme, "East St. Louis Toodle-O." His mixture of songs and tempos was excellent. I had heard most of his standards such as "In A Sentimental Mood," "Mood Indigo" and "Solitude" several hundred times in person or on records. But I had not had the pleasure of hearing "Harmony In Harlem," "Ridin' A Blue Note," or Rex Stewart's interpretations of

"Jeep's Blues" and "Trumpets In Spain."

By 1 a.m. on the morning of August 27, the Ellington band was jamming a 12-bar nameless "gut bucket" blues tune at a medium tempo. The rhythm section was pushing the band to the point that they were virtually rocking the building's foundation and lifting the roof off the Coliseum. Every member of the band, including Fred Guy on guitar, soloed at least three choruses or more. The jam session among the members of the band lasted an hour or more past closing hour. The session was not recorded but it was a forerunner of things to come like the Newport Jazz Festival in 1956 when Paul Gonsalves blew 27 choruses of "Diminuendo And Crescendo In Blue." Almost 60 years have passed since that memorable morning, however the performance is one that will be etched in my memory until I make my final exit.

Duke stayed in Chicago after the Exposition and opened in the Panther Room of the Sherman Hotel on September 4. It was most unfortunate that I did not have an opportunity to hear that performance, except on radio. The only Negroes permitted in downtown hotels were the colored people who worked in them such as maids, porters and musicians. Sad, but true, little had changed except the visible chains and the frequent lynchings 75 years after the Emancipation Proclamation had been signed by President Abraham Lincoln.

Dempsey J. Travis and Louie Bellson taken on June 31,1983, at the Holiday Day Inn on Lake Shore Drive in Chicago.

12 - VIEWS OF THE DUKE THROUGH THE EYES OF LOUIE BELLSON

In March, 1951, Johnny Hodges, Lawrence Brown and Sonny Greer quit the Ellington Orchestra at the same time. Collectively, the three had been with the Ellington organizations for a total of 73 years. Their departures left a void in the orchestra and marked another low point in the Duke's career, the others being the losses of his mother in 1935 and his father in 1937.

Duke's mother always told him as a child not to worry about directions when he reached various crossroads in life because there would always be someone there to tell him the right way to go. At this fork in the road the people who showed him the way were Juan and Rosebud Tizol, Ellington's former trombone player and his wife. Tizol told Duke that all he had to do was give the word, and that he, Louie Bellson and Willie Smith would leave the Harry James Orchestra, after giving James the customary two weeks' notice.

Willie Smith, second from left, and Louie Bellson, on drums at rear, in May, 1951, shortly after joining the Ellington Band.

Willie Smith was an alumnus of the Jimmie Lunceford Orchestra and one of the world's greatest lead alto saxophone players; Louie Bellson, prior to joining Harry James, had been a star precision drummer for both the Tommy Dorsey and Benny Goodman Orchestras.

Under ordinary circumstances the Duke would not have considered taking men from a fellow band leaders' orchestra. It was considered unethical, but in this case he did not feel any pain because Harry James had snatched Tizol, a brilliant trombone player, out of the Ellington band seven years earlier in April, 1944.

Harry James, orchestra leader and former trumpet star with Benny Goodman.

Harry James did not exactly jump up and down and click his heels when he received the notice that three of his best players were leaving his orchestra to join Duke Ellington. On the other hand, he did not show any bitterness. As a matter of fact he said, "It is not every day that one gets an opportunity to play with Duke Ellington's Great Orchestra. Therefore, you guys can go with my blessing."

In May, 1951, when Bellson joined the Ellington Orchestra, Billy Strayhorn was his assigned roommate. Billy did not travel with the band more than a week or two at a time and then he would go back to New York to busy himself with writing arrangements and compose music for the orchestra.

When Billy went back to New York City, following Bellson's first week with the band, Duke suggested that Louie share a room with him. Bellson thought it was an excellent idea because this would give him an opportunity to ask some questions like: "How did you do the voicing in 'Caravan' for the reeds and the brass? The arrangement is so poetic I could figuratively see a caravan of camels coming across the horizon in the desert sand."

It did not take long for Bellson to realize that the Ellington method of orchestrating was secret information shared by only two men, the Duke and Billy. Neither of them would share information with anyone else because it was their own personal home grown musical recipe.

The first night Bellson shared a hotel room with Ellington was not so bad. Duke stayed up all of that night writing. However, when the big man fell asleep he was knocked out like a fighter who had caught a Joe Louis left hook to the head. You literally had to pull Duke out of the bed by his feet to wake him up. In contrast, the soft tingle of the doorbell or telephone would instantly awaken Bellson. All through the night Bellson found himself responding to voices on the other side of the door bellowing: "Flowers for Mr. Ellington" or "Telegrams for Mr. Ellington." This kind of traffic for the very popular Mr. Ellington was par for the course. By the seventh day, Bellson realized that he could not effectively perform on his drums without getting at least six hours of uninterrupted sleep. It was at this point that Bellson told Duke he had to have his own room, Duke put his arms around Bellson's shoulders and jovially said: "You got it."

During the week that Bellson shared space with the Duke, he got some insight into how the great man handled interruptions during the course of a 24-hour day. Flowers, telegrams and people poured into the Duke's suite and dressing room all day, like marchers in a Veterans' Day parade. Then there were those 50-plus-year-old girls who would just drop by to say hello for old times' sake. Duke never brushed or slighted anyone. He created time for everybody, young and the old, rich and the poor, famous and the want-to-be-famous.

Duke Ellington's appetite for beautiful women, expensive clothes and fine food was expensive. His breakfast, usually served in his hotel room in mid-afternoon, would include a 12-ounce broiled steak with vegetables and a garden salad on the side. His liquids included a large jar of fruit juice in addition to a 32-ounce pitcher of plain hot water. He always insisted, in the strongest terms, that hot water be served with his first meal of the day.

Duke proved that the size of his legendary appetite had not been exaggerated when he went on the road with the "Big Show of '51." Mrs. "Curly" Balassoni, Bellson's mother, gave a dinner party at their home in Moline, Illinois. Invited guests were the entire Ellington Orchestra plus the stage show cast that included Nat Cole, Sarah Vaughan, Patterson and Jackson, Timmie Rogers, and Peg Leg Bates.

Mrs. Balassoni cooked 10 turkeys and an enormous quantity of food. Duke Ellington ate a whole turkey by himself and said: "I paced that gorgeous feast with the proper salad punctuations, and I came off the champ. Everybody else thought that every course was the main course. I was alone in the dining room and sitting tall when the desserts were served."

The unforgettable Nat "King" Cole in 1951.

Sarah "The Devine One" Vaughan. For her no note was too high or too low.

Mrs. Balassoni was a beautiful human being like her son Louie. Moline, Illinois, was the Selma, Alabama of the North in the 1950's. They would not permit Negroes to sleep in the hotels or eat in the restaurants. A white woman giving a dinner party for a group of Negroes in an all-white community in that town was performing a courageous life-threatening act. She stands alone in a class by herself.

Duke was also alone and in a class by himself when it came to respecting the individuality of the musicians who joined his band. For example, when Bellson became a member of the Ellington group, Duke did not say "Bellson, I want you to play and sound like Sonny Greer." Right from the top he said: "I want to hear you." Then he would commence writing arrangements that would showcase the player's capabilities.

After Bellson had been with the band about six months, Duke remarked: "I understand from Juan Tizol and Willie Smith that you are a first-class writer and arranger. I would like to see some of your work."

Bellson found it embarrassing to have to show his arrangements

99

to Ellington and Strayhorn, two of the best arrangers and writers on the continent. After Duke asked about his work a third time, Juan Tizol insisted that Bellson let Duke see his charts. The two numbers that Bellson surrendered to Ellington were "Skin Deep" and "The Hawk Talks." Duke liked the material and he recorded both of the numbers within a couple of weeks.

Through observation, Bellson noted that Ellington and Strayhorn never put endings of any of their compositions or arrangements on regular score paper. They would have everything on manuscript up to W or the last four bars of a song and then they stop in mid-stream. The final four bars would be completed on the bandstand or in the rehearsal hall. Duke would say, "Fellows, here is what we are going to do to finish the number. Johnny you take this note, "Cootie" you take that note, and so forth. And we will end it on the third beat." Duke would raise and then lower his arms and the orchestra would strike a chord that sounded like it was made in heaven.

When Duke Ellington was writing his first sacred concert, based on the first three words of the first chapter of the Book of Genesis, he had to match his music with the message.

In the process of planting a biblical seed, he approached LouiseBellson and told him that he wanted him to play a drum solo in church. The expression on Bellson's face revealed that he was puzzled by the request because in his church playing drums would not even be considered.

Bellson queried, "Duke, How do you do that?" Duke smiled and walked away without answering the question. Two days later, Ellington cornered Bellson again and said, "You know the music that I am writing is based on the Bible. In the beginning we had thunder. In the beginning we had lighting, you are both."

Duke gave this appraisal of the Sacred Concert: "All the members of the band played in character. Cootie Williams growled, Cat Anderson sent notes flying around the roof, Louie Bellson was indeed thunder and lighting, and very elegant in his percussion declaration, Harry Carney stated the theme with power and dignity, Johnny Hodges sang "Come Sunday" through his horn as only he could...."

A love bug struck Louie Bellson and singer Pearl Bailey early in 1953 and they got married in London. Bellson subsequently left the Ellington Orchestra to organize a band to back up his inimitable wife, sometimes known as Pearlly Mae.

Duke and Bellson stayed in close touch with each other after

Louie left the Ellington Orchestra, and Bellson frequently returned to play with the orchestra when there was a need for his services and he could adjust his schedule. As matter of fact, when Sonny Payne was sick, Bellson postponed a gig in Sweden and played a four-week job at Birdland in New York with Ellington.

Pearl Bailey and Louie Bellson were married in London, England, in January, 1953. Shortly after that, Bellson resigned from the Ellington group. He organized a band to support his wife's act.

Bellson felt as if Duke was his second father. When Duke got sick, Pearl Bailey said, "Louie, your father is dead. Duke is your father now. Why don't you get on a plane and go and see him?"

Bellson retorted: "Why don't I? I did not call ahead to say I was coming. But on Thursday, April 4,1974, I told the people at NBC I was going to see Duke and got on a plane. I went directly from the airport to the hospital."

When Bellson reached the hospital, he was told he could not go up and see Duke Ellington. But one of the people working at the reception desk recognized Bellson and called up to the Duke's floor and talked to somebody at the nursing station near his room.

Overhearing Bellson's name being mentioned, Duke said: "Have him come up right away."

Bellson remembers,"Duke had been lying down. So they sat him up in a chair. He looked really sick, but I did not know the degree.

Over in the corner of the room I saw a little Wurlitzer electric piano which he always carried with him. When I saw that it made me feel good because I figured he was thinking about doing some writing.

Bellson adds: "The next day when I went to see him they would not permit me to stay more than 10 minutes because he became tired very easily. After spending a couple minutes in his room, I left and went down to the gift shop and bought him a beautiful blue sweater. That was his favorite color. It was a birthday gift because I knew I would not be able to come back for his natal day, which was April 29. Before leaving the room for the last time I said, pointing to the Wurlitzer in the corner of the room, 'It looks like you are going to be doing some composing.' He said 'Nope,' I had never heard him say anything negative. It was then that I knew in my heart I had heard the last chord." Duke died May 24,1974.

Al Hibbler and Ed Sullivan, the columnist and host of the Toast of The Town (1948-1971), a one-hour Sunday night CBS television variety show. Hibbler was paid for $5,000 for one performance on that show in 1952. In 1956 Sullivan paid Elvis Presley $50,000 for three performances.

13 - DUKE WAS AL HIBBLER'S LUCKY SO AND SO

Duke's first encounter with Albert George Hibbler was in Little Rock, Arkansas, in 1935. Hibbler auditioned with the Ellington band but was not hired. After the session, Ellington pulled Al Hibbler aside and whispered, "I can handle a blind man, but I cannot handle a blind drunk. Kid you are not ready. You'd better go back to 9th Street."

Hibbler hung around Little Rock for approximately another year before going to Memphis to work with Dave Jenkins and his playmates. In May of 1939 the Clifford Douglas Band, known as "Boots" and his buddies out of San Antonio, rolled into Memphis to play several one-night stands. Hibbler hooked up with them and went on a road tour. The young man packed all of his worldly belongings in a small straw suitcase and moved to San Antonio with the "Boots" outfit on the promise of steady work. He stayed in the small city for two years.

"Dizzy" Gillespie and Dempsey J. Travis doing an interview and radio show on WBEZ 91.5 F.M. in Chicago.

The Jay McShann Orchestra from Kansas City featuring Charlie "Yard Bird" Parker on alto sax was touring Texas in late 1941. Parker had heard about Hibbler being in San Antonio through John "Dizzy" Gillespie and Don Redman. When the band reached

San Antonio, Parker looked up Hibbler and found that he was available and willing to travel. Parker told Jay McShann to hire Hibbler and take him to New York City to open with the band at the Savoy Ballroom, "The Home Of Happy Feet."

McShann recoiled at Charlie Parker's suggestion and said: "I don't want no blind s.o.b. in my band. I don't want that responsibility."

"Yard Bird" replied: "If you don't hire Hibbler, I quit." Hibbler was hired.

When Hibbler opened at the Savoy with the McShann orchestra, he got very good reviews from the Negro press. After they closed at the Savoy, the band went on a theater road tour of Colored movie houses, commencing with the Apollo Theater in New York City, Earl Theater in Philadelphia, the Royal Theater in Baltimore, the Howard Theater in Washington, the Paradise Theater in Detroit, and finally the Regal Theater in Chicago. These theaters were known among Colored musicians as the "Chitterling" Circuit.

Al Hibbler is third from the left in the second row;. Jay McShann is at the piano.

Hibbler quit Jay McShann's Orchestra in January, 1943, to go out on his first independent venture. He got a job at Pemberton's Hollywood Cabaret in New York City and on weekends doubled by working a second gig at Monroe's Uptown House, an after-hours joint that did not start jumping until 2 a.m.

On Saturday, May 15,1943, Hibbler and Duke Ellington's paths crossed again at the Hurricane Club at 49th and Broadway in New York City. Duke obviously had forgotten Hibbler's 1935 audition with his band in Little Rock. However, Duke's vibes were positive when told by Mary Lou Williams, an Ellington staff arranger and former pianist with the Andy Kirk Orchestra, and her husband, Harold "Shorty" Baker, a trumpet player with Ellington, that Al Hibbler was downstairs bending his elbow at a bar called the Turf. They also hinted that there was an outside possibility of getting Hibbler to come up and sing. "Bring him up," Duke said. They brought Al Hibbler upstairs to sing several songs, including "Summertime," "Trees," and "Solitude." Duke was more than pleased with what he had heard; Hibbler's "Trees" rendition knocked him out.

Part of the Ellington Orchestra at the Hurricane Club in New York City in 1943. Right to left: Junior Raglin, Ben Webster, Nat Jones and Jimmy Hamilton. Joe "Tricky Sam" Nanton is soloing on his trombone.

Duke writes in his biography "Music Is My Mistress": "The thought of adding another singer to the payroll was a cause of concern; a smart businessman would not have considered it. But me - well, my ears make decisions." Duke already had three singers on his payroll: Kay Davis, who later married Edward D. Wimp Jr., a successful Chicago businessman; Marie Ellington, who subsequently married the immortal Nat "King" Cole, and Joya Sherrill.

After the set, Duke told Hibbler, "I like your style, you just started to work."

Hibbler obviously failed to understand what Duke had said about his being hired because he told the writer, "I was hanging out with the band for two weeks and I did not know that I had been hired at a salary of $250 per week. This was a long way up the scale from the $2.50 a week I was making as a singer in Little Rock in 1936."

Al had been coming down to the Hurricane every night for two weeks to sing with Ellington's band but he had not received the first crust of bread. Hib was stone broke and was really in need of money. However, every time he would ask Duke about some dough, Duke would reply, "Do nothing till you hear from me."

"Do Nothing Till You Hear From Me" was an Ellington-coined phrase that became the title of Bob Russell's 1943 lyrical version of Duke's "Concerto For Cootie," written in 1939.

Duke partying after hours with Johnny Hartman, the great singer; Phyllis Branch, entertainer; Herman Roberts, owner of Roberts Show Lounge in Chicago, and Hibbler seated next to Ellington.

Ellington later said, "It was much easier than I thought it would be for Hibbler to learn songs. The reason was because he was gifted with ears that could see, and so miracles happened. Hib learned song after song, and soon he was our major asset - truly a profitable investment, both dollar-wise and for the luxury of keeping my ears in deep fat..."

Duke evaluated Hibbler's talents as stratospheric, saying, "Hib has so many sounds that even without words he can tell of fantasy beyond fantasy. Hib's great dramatic devices and the variety of tonal changes give him almost unlimited range. His capabilities are many, but I should mention first that he had clear, understandable enunciation. He could produce a whispering confidential sound or an outburst that borders on panic. He will adopt a nasal tone at just the right word or note, or affect a sudden drop in what sounds like the below-compass bass. Cries, laughs, and highly animated calls - he uses them all to make the listener see it as he sees it...."

Ellington and Hibbler had a mutual admiration society in that they displayed a great deal of respect and fondness for each other. Duke treated Hibbler and Strayhorn more like sons than he did Mercer Ellington. Hibbler sang with the Ellington organization for eight and a half years, a longevity exceeded only by 11 years for vocalist Ivie Anderson.

Duke Ellington and Ken Blewett, manager of the Regal Theater, conferring backstage as they lean on the baby grand piano.

Hibbler, during his tenure with Ellington, saw many sides of the man. He learned that Duke was very religious. As evidence of this Hibbler recalls, "We were playing at the Regal Theater in Chicago. On this particular day, I was in my dressing room bent over, resting my arms on the dressing table and holding my aching head because I had been out boozing and chasing the girls all the night before.

"A Jehovah's Witness by the name of Miss Fitzgerald and known by Mr. Ellington knocked on my dressing room door and said, 'I would like to talk to you about God.'

"I bellowed, 'Woman, get away from my door. I don't feel like talking about nothing.'

"Duke, whose dressing room was next to mine, knocked on the wall and said, 'Did I hear you say what I thought you said?'

"I snapped, 'I don't know what you thought you heard, but whatever it was, I said it.'

"Duke dashed into my dressing room, pulled up a chair, put both of his legs across my legs and pinned me down."

"Ellington, in a hushed but angry tone, warned, 'Don't you ever let me hear you say a thing like that again.'

Duke hams it up for Tony Bennett backstage at the Regal Theater.

"'Have you ever seen God? How do you know she is not God?' Duke challenged. 'If you don't respect God, who do you respect? I believe that if you respect God, God will respect you.'"

Ellington validated his feelings about God and religion in the two sacred concerts he wrote almost two decades after that exchange he had about God with Al Hibbler in the dressing room of the Regal Theater.

It was at the Regal in 1946 that the writer first saw and heard Al Hibbler sing in person. I would not have known he was blind from his posture and the assurance he reflected in his walk. There was no sign of groping or doubt in his brisk and confident movement.

What I did not know until Hibbler told me some years later was that Duke had worked out a formula for him getting on and off the stage with dignity. Duke would stand midstage at the microphone saying nice things about Hibbler, and when he said "Albert George" that was the key for Al Hibbler to start walking directly toward the sound of Duke's voice. Duke would continue the chatter until Hibbler reached the mike. Their shoulders would barely touch as Duke moved off center stage. When Hibbler finished his performance, he would be guided off by the voice of Duke Ellington, who was talking to Hibbler at a level just above a whisper from the theater wings.

Ray Nance, a Chicago Wendell Phillips High School grad who became a triple threat musician with Duke. He was an excellent trumpeter and violinist and he both sang and danced with flash and style.

Laurie, a lady love who had been Hibbler's traveling companion, one day was not waiting in the wings with Duke. She had hopped on a plane and flown away, and Hibbler was showing some real signs of grief and depression. Duke attempted to console him on a train ride enroute to San Francisco from Los Angeles. During the anguished and tearful five-hour conversation on the train, Duke implied more than once that the woman had not been as faithful as Hibbler had believed. Therefore, Duke suggested that Hib dry his tears and celebrate the departure of an unfaithful lover by recording Ellington's 1945 composition, "I'm Just A Lucky So And So."

In Baltimore, Hibbler was not such a lucky so-and-so when he was treated like a black mongrel by a white female clerk and a policeman. The Ellington Orchestra was playing at the Lord Baltimore Hotel when Hibbler and Ray Nance decided to go down to the hotel drug store and have a Coke. When they sat down at the counter and asked for a Coca Cola, the counter girl snapped, "Get outa here, you know we don't serve no niggers."

Ray Nance bristled and shot back, "I don't eat or drink them either."

The counter girl replied, "You are smart niggers, I'm going to call the police." On her cue, a cop rushed in like a Nazi storm trooper and roared, "Give them niggers the Cokes, but they better not attempt to drink that Coke in this drug store, if they do, I'm going to take that bottle and wear their goddam nigger heads out with it."

The Ellington group was able to avoid a great deal of racial humiliation because band members ate, drank and slept in their own private Pullman cars. In spite of this safety net, the Ellington people, like whales, had to come up for air from time to time. Often they had to inhale the racist soot that permeated every one of the 48 states. Oklahoma, the 46th state to be admitted to the Union in 1907 was no less racist than Maryland, the seventh state admitted in 1788.

The Ellington Orchestra was playing a three-night gig at a club in Oklahoma City and the four singers, Hibbler, Marie Ellington, Kay Davis and Joya Sherrill were sitting in front near the band-stand at a cabaret-style table. A white policeman came into the club and saw Kay Davis, a very light complexion Colored woman sitting with three Colored people of a darker skin tone. The cop asked Ellington, "What is that white girl doing sitting down there with two nigger girls and one nigger boy? You are asking for trouble if you don't remove those three niggers from the table."

Duke replied, "What white woman?" The cop growled, "You know what woman," pointing to Kay Davis. Duke countered, "Man, that is no white woman; she is one of us." The officer snapped, "She looks white," demanding that Duke send the three "niggers" back to the dressing room. Duke called his road manager, Jack Boyd, who was white, to escort Kay back to the stage wing where she waited for her time to perform.

Hibbler's performance was always at the top of his game, but Ellington had never raised his initial weekly salary of $250. When Hibbler asked Duke to give him a $50 a week raise, Duke asked: "Do you think you are Bing Crosby or Frank Sinatra?"

The two men never reached a meeting of the minds on money so Hibbler left the Duke on Monday, July 9,1951. For almost a year after he left, he was being booked as: "Al Hibbler, formerly with the Duke Ellington Orchestra." He did well promoting himself in that fashion until that dog stop biting. His basic income today is derived from Social Security and recording royalties.

Several days after Duke died, on May 24,1974, Hibbler called Mercer Ellington and announced, "I am coming to the funeral."

"Yes, I was hoping you would come," Mercer replied. "I'll send a limousine to pick you up."

Hibbler asked, "Do you want me to do a number?"

Mercer: "I want you to sing 'Trees'".

Hibbler attended Duke's funeral which drew more than 10,000 mourners. Al was seated with such dignitaries as William Warfield, Jack Dempsey, Mary Lou Williams, Gordon Parks, Earl Hines, Joya Sherril, Count Basie, Dorothy Donegan, Dick Gregory, Pearl Bailey, Ray Nance, Billy Taylor and Louie Bellson, among others. Hibbler was never called on to sing "Trees."

Ellington's eulogy was delivered by Stanley Dance, his long-time friend and biographer; actor Brock Peters recited poetry; Ray Nance performed on the violin; McHenry Boatwright sang and Ella Fitzgerald delivered a vocal tribute to Ellington. Joe Williams sang "Come Sunday," a 1945 Duke Ellington composition, in final praise of the Duke.

Clark Terry and Dempsey J. Travis, author, in the
dressing room at Chicago's Orchestra Hall on
December 29,1995.

14 - CLARK TERRY: AN ELLINGTONION UNIVERSITY CUM LAUDE GRAD

Clark Terry, the seventh of ten children (seven girls and three boys), was born in St. Louis, in the 12th month on the 14th day and in the 20th year of the 20th century. His family was poorer than the proverbial church mice, and in order to relieve the financial strain on his mother and father, Terry moved in with his oldest sister and her husband when he was 9 years old, earning his room and board by hauling ashes from potbellied stoves for people in the neighborhood. An articulate and friendly young boy, Clark Terry was what is called real cheap labor because he only charged pennies for his services. He promoted his hauling business by passing out self-made handbills inscribed: "Let the Terry Brothers Do Your Hauling."

Sy, his sister's husband, was a tuba player with the Dewey Jackson band, known as the Musical Ambassadors, one of the top bands in the St. Louis area at that time. Sy was a great tuba player, one of the best who ever came out of the river city. The Jackson band rehearsed at Sy's house and of course young Terry hung around and listened, leading him to dig jazz very early in life. He became very closely attached to Louis Caldwell, a trumpet player in the Dewey Jackson band. Caldwell was extra nice to little Clark, bringing him candy every time the band rehearsed. Terry even now remembers vividly the Mary Janes that Caldwell frequently gave him. Mary Janes were a yellow caramel chewy candy, a favorite among the kids back in the late 1920's and 30's. In addition to the candy, Mr. Caldwell gave him a couple of pennies to watch his horn when the band took a break.

Clark Terry remembers that once Louis Caldwell came back from his 15-minute break sooner than expected and he caught the kid trying desperately to get a sound out of his trumpet. The kid was huffing and puffing trying to get a sound, any sound, to come out. Caldwell said, "Son, you're going to be a trumpet player!" That compliment inspired Terry and he has ever since hung in there with the trumpet family.

Radio helped young Terry's musical education. He used to put his little radio in a large fishbowl to give it a bigger sound. Kids in the community used to try to imitate the sounds of the big bands that they heard on the radio by creating make-shift instruments. Clark's brother wanted to play drums and since he could not afford to buy a set he devised a drum out of a worn-out large dish pan, the kind used to catch ice drippings from huge blocks of ice pushed into the top of the ice box several times a week. The ice box is what everyone used to keep food from spoiling before we had refrigerators.

Terry's brother placed the old ice pan on top of a tall, upside-down pyramid-shaped bushel basket, making it into an excellent snare drum. His brother used old chair rungs as substitutes for drumsticks. To get a tuba sound, the kids took a big, round tin beer mug, wrapped a vacuum hose around it, blew through it, and got fantastic bass noises.

Clark made a trumpet by coiling an old hose and putting a kerosene funnel on one end to look like the bell of a trumpet and a pipe on the other end for a mouthpiece. Admittedly the contraption didn't look very musical, but it actually produced a sound like a trumpet, according to Terry.

Clark Terry didn't get his first real musical instrument until he reached Vashon High School, a St. Louis secondary school for colored children located on Garrison and McLead in St. Louis. He registered for the band on his first day in high school because he wanted to learn to play a real trumpet. Clarence Hydon Wilson, the bandmaster, said to him, "I understand you want to play the trumpet. I'm sorry, we don't have a single trumpet left. But I've got an old valve trombone hanging over there on the wall that you can use." Mr. Wilson assured young Terry that the fingering on that instrument was exactly like a B-flat trumpet. "You can make a lot of noise with it." He added: "Take it and get the heck out of my face."

Clark took the trombone home and went to work on it. He got his fingering together because like Mr. Wilson had said the fingering was exactly like that of a B-flat trumpet. He never became proficient on the trombone but he learned to appreciate the instrument. Clark recalls that Mr. Wilson was an excellent music teacher and that he kept young Terry right under his wing until the senior year when the economics of the great Depression dictated that the Terry brothers had to drop out of school to chip in full time and help their father and unmarried sisters.

Terry quickly got involved in playing jazz as a profession when his brother-in-law took him on his first gig. Sy later introduced Clark to another band that was known as Dollar Bill and his Small Change in which Clark was initially one of the pennies. He eventually worked his way up to be a nickel. Later he played with Fate Marable, a giant among musicians in the St. Louis area.

Terry's first road gig was with Willie Austin, a trombone player and bandleader from St. Louis traveling with the Reuben & Cherry Carnival Show. Carnival and medicine shows during the big economic catastrophe of the 1930's were a means of survival for many musicians. Both Roy Eldridge and Harry James got early experience working with these carnival shows.

The Reuben & Cherry Carnival Show was a big opportunity for Clark until it went bankrupt in Hattiesburg, Mississippi. There they were, stranded without any money in the middle of cottonland where most sharecroppers traded at plantation owned stores using scrip in lieu of dollars. In the 1960's, 100 years after emancipation, Dr. Martin Luther King, Jr., discovered that many sharecroppers had never seen U.S. currency in their cotton-picking lives.

Luckily, a fellow with the carnival who had a monkey act also owned a truck and Willie Austin was able to con the man into letting him and his lady ride in the cab of his truck, Clark and a couple of the other musicians rode in the rear of the truck with 15 active monkeys for 750 miles. That, Clark recalls, was a real experience. During the course of the trip, band members learned to know the monkeys by their names and Clark claims that the monkeys knew them by theirs.

The next time Clark Terry hit the road was with a big-time blues singer by the name of Ida Cox who headed her Dark Town Scandal Show. It was a great experience for the young musician. They used to travel in an old, broken-down bus and every time they came to a hill everybody had to get out and push. A midget called "Prince" in the show just sat in the bus while the rest of the guys pushed. Ida Cox asked him one day, "What are you doing sitting in the bus while we are all out here pushing?"

He answered: "I'm too small to push."

Ida retorted, "We've got a tiny place for you to push here at the back of the bus."

Clark has never forgotten that; Ida's sense of humor always cracked him up.

When the Cox show terminated in St.Louis, Clark got a regular gig with Fate Marable who had one of the most celebrated river-boat bands of the day. Marable had employed as guest stars such luminaries as Louis Armstrong. Fate himself was quite a character who had changed his name from Marble to Marable. "Whenever Fate was going to fire a person," Terry recounts, "he'd take one of the fire axes from the wall of the boat and put it in that cat's seat. When the guy came on board, we would start playing. Naturally the cat would figure he was late, and as he ran up to the band, we would break into playing 'There'll be Some Changes Made.'" Clark believes to this day that "getting the axe" as an expression for getting fired was actually coined by Fate Marable of St. Louis.

Ida Cox, a great blues singer with a rich contralto voice. When this woman sang the blues, there were strong implications.

In 1942, Clark signed up with a Navy recruiter in St. Louis and was shipped directly to Great Lakes Naval Training Center, approximately 40 miles north of Chicago. During the next three years, he played with the Navy All-Star Band under the direction of Willie Smith, former altoist with the Jimmie Lunceford Orchestra. Some of the musical cats who passed through Great Lakes were Dave Young, the tenor sax player formerly with Fletcher Henderson and Roy Eldridge; Pee Wee Jackson, trumpeter with Earl Hines and Jimmie Lunceford, and Lonnie Simmons, tenor sax player with Fats Waller, the Savoy Sultons and the Ella Fitzgerald Orchestra. With those star players, Clark had a terrific jazz experience in the United States Navy.

After Terry was discharged in 1945, he worked with the Lionel Hampton's band for three weeks and then he went back to St. Louis to spend the next 18 months as the straw boss and lead trumpet player with the George Hudson band. Hudson had built a solid reputation with his house band at

Dave Young, tenor sax player with Fletcher Henderson and Roy Eldridge Orchestras.

the "for whites only" Club Plantation which was to St. Louis what the Cotton Club was to New York's Harlem and the Grand Terrace to the South Side of Chicago. George Hudson selected a number of musicians who were serious about their craft: Singleton Palmer on string bass; Weasel Parker on tenor sax, and trumpeter Clark Terry. When new acts came into the club, Hudson would rehearse their music as if it were his own. Performers loved the band because they played their music right. Many of them told members of the Hudson orchestra that they had never heard their music played so beautifully. Conscientiousness paid off because entertainers spread the word about how well the George Hudson orchestra performed and therefore the band's reputation had preceded it to New York's Apollo Theater in 1946. Their little tenor man, Willie "Weasel" Parker, played such a bad solo on "Body and Soul" during the first show at the Apollo that Illinois Jacquet, a big star at the time, ran backstage and told Jack Schiffman, the owner of the Apollo, that he had to "Take it out! Take that number out!" The tenor man in George Hudson's band was just that good.

In 1947, while Clark was still working with George Hudson at the Club Plantation in St. Louis, he received a call from Charlie Barnet, the millionaire orchestra leader who played music for kicks in Los Angeles. Barnet told Clark that his good friend Gerald Wilson had recommended him highly and he wanted to know whether Terry would be interested in joining the orchestra playing at Hermosa Beach. Clark told him that he would love to, and Barnet asked him if he wanted to drive, fly or take the train. Clark told him that he wanted to take the train so he would have time to think about the gig while traveling. He did not want to rush into

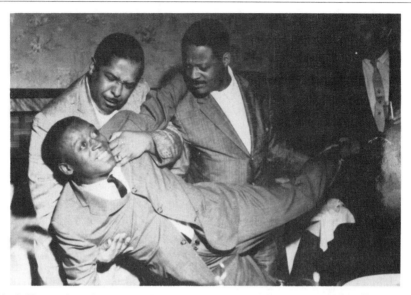

Clark Terry clowning around with Miles Davis and Lonnie Simmons, the former tenor sax player with Fats Waller, Savoy Sultons, Chick Webb and Ella Fitzgerald.

anything too fast. Barnet eagerly sent him a ticket by airmail special delivery. Terry had a three-day train ride to contemplate his future. Gerald Wilson met him at the station and took him directly to Hermosa Beach where the Charlie Barnet band was performing. They were on the air in the middle of a coast-to-coast radio broadcast when Clark walked up to the bandstand. Charlie Barnet signaled for Clark to take his horn out of the case. Barnet then announced on the air, "And now, our new trumpet player, Clark Terry." Clark had to go right into a number, the name of which he can't recall, but he does remember it was a number that had a standard set of chord changes like maybe "Lady Be Good." Once he heard the first chorus, he was home free. "That was Charlie Barnet's style of doing things," Clark Terry recalls. "Charlie Barnet is a beautiful man." In fact, the two men are still the best of friends. Barnet's mother Charlotte owned considerable stock in the New York Central Railroad, and when she died, all of the money went to Charlie. After that Barnet used to give the guys in the band presents of Buicks, Cadillacs and Packards for Christmas. But when Clark joined the band Charlie was only giving out fifths of whiskey. That was the story of his life. Some of the guys who had been with the Barnet band earlier said that Charlie ran through a million dollars in a very short time. In addition to giving big gifts, he paid astronomical salaries.

In 1948, Count Basie asked Clark Terry to join his band. Clark

Charlie Barnet, the independently wealthy orchestra leader who played music for kicks.

had not worked with Basie long before the Count began to encounter financial problems. Count Basie's managing agent in New York told him that he had to reduce the size of his band immediately. Clark returned to St. Louis but had only been there a short time when he received another call from the Count asking him to rejoin the band at the Brass Rail in Chicago on the northwest corner of Randolph and Dearborn just a half block west of the Oriental Theater. Basie told Terry to bring along a good tenor man. Clark brought along Bob Graff, to a young white tenor sax player from St. Louis. Other musicians in the group were Freddie Green on guitar, Gus Johnson on drums, Jimmy Lewis on bass, and Buddy DeFranco on clarinet with the Count on piano. Joe Williams was the vocalist for two months.

When Bob Graff was recruited by Woody Herman, he was replaced with Waddell Gray. Basie left Chicago and went back to New York and apparently resolved his financial problems because in less than six months he started reorganizing his big band. While the band was playing at the Strand Theater in New York City, Basie let it be known that he needed another alto sax player. Clark told him that he had a friend in St. Louis who could fill the bill. Count said, "Call him up."

Clark promptly called Ernie Wilkins, who had never played an alto sax in his life. Clark very quietly asked, "Can you get an alto?

Do you want to come and join Basie?" Ernie borrowed a silver-colored high school student's saxophone (they used to call them the "grey ghosts") and came to New York the next day. The Basie band was still playing out of its old Kansas City arrangement book, so Clark suggested that Basie should let Ernie Wilkins write some new material. That might have been the best suggestion Terry ever made because from that point on the band's reputation simply skyrocketed. Ernie wrote great material for the band and for vocalist Joe Williams. All of those good things came as a result of one whispered telephone call!

In 1951 Duke Ellington dropped in on one of Count Basie's gigs

The Count Basie Band at the Brass Rail in Chicago. From left: Count Basie, Jimmy Lewis, Buddy DeFranco, Gus Johnson, Wardell Gray, Freddie Green, Clark Terry.

to scout. Duke subsequently had his managing agent work out a deal whereby Clark Terry would leave Count Basie purportedly because he was tired and needed some rest. The agent agreed to pay Clark $200 per week while he rested in St. Louis. This subterfuge was used because Duke would not dare lift a musician out of his good buddy's orchestra.

Incidentally, the Count had just given Clark Terry a $10 raise making his salary a "grand" total of $125 per week, Basie immediately revoked that raise when Clark handed him his notice.

Clark Terry was officially enrolled in the University of Ellingtonism in November, 1951, Duke immediately made a big boy out of Clark when he threw him into one of the most awesome trumpet sections in the nation: William "Cat" Anderson, Harold "Shorty" Baker and Ray "Little Dipper" Nance. All of those cats had their acts together. Clark considered the Barnet and Basie orchestras primary and secondary schools when compared with the sophisticated Ellington's curriculum.

Duke Ellington never wrote parts like first, second, third or fourth trumpet; he simply wrote Anderson, Nance, Baker and Clark. Those were the parts. You didn't know whether or not it was first, second, third or fourth until you actually played it. He started this system back in the early days of his orchestra because he found that Rex Stewart had an uncanny way of playing an E-natural on the horn. Stewart used to play it with a semi- or suppressed valve, which is called a cock-valve. Therefore, whenever this note appeared in a chord, Duke automatically gave it to

Clark Terry officially joined the Ellington Orchestra in November, 1951.

Stewart. It didn't matter whether it was first, second, third or fourth, so one's part could jump all over the place. Duke's band was his instrument. It's true. Duke surrounded himself with talented musicians whom he dug, and he used them to extend his feelings musically.

Clark Terry makes this observation, "Duke had a way of getting things out of you that you didn't realize you had in you. Let me give you an example. We were doing a album called "The Drum is a Woman," and Duke came to me saying, "Clark, I want you to play Buddy Bolden for me on this album."

I said, "Maestro, I don't know who the hell Buddy Bolden is!"

Duke said, "Oh, sure you know Buddy Bolden. Buddy Bolden was suave, handsome and a debonair cat the ladies loved. And he was fantastic! He was fabulous, he was always sought after. He had the biggest, fattest trumpet sound in town. He bent notes to the ninth degree. He used to tune up in New Orleans and break glass in Algiers! He was great with diminishes. When he played a diminish, he bent those notes man like you have never heard them before.'

"By this time, Duke had me psyched out! He finished by saying: 'as a matter of fact, you are Buddy Bolden!' So I thought I was Buddy Bolden.

Duke said, "Play Buddy Bolden for this record date."

I played it and at the conclusion of the session, Duke came up to me and put his arms around my shoulders, and said, "That was Buddy Bolden."

Clark added: "That Duke wants life and music to always be in a state of being born. He never wrote the final rites to a composition. The maestro would frequently ask members of the orchestra to come up with some ideas for the final four closing bars. He would then play around with several of the suggested closing. The one he selected would always sound like there was more to come."

Clark Terry wrote a boppish ending to Ellington "Newport Festival Suite" played at Newport late on the evening of July 8, 1956. The suite was followed on the program with an Ellington rendition of his own 1937 composition of "Diminuendo and Crescendo in Blue." In the bridge of the song there was supposed to be a brief blues solo. Instead Paul Gonsalves opened up and started wailing several red-hot choruses and then the audience joined in by clapping their hands to the beat and dancing in the aisle. Duke got caught in the whirl of the solo in the seventh chorus and he started clapping his hands and making abbreviated dance steps and hollering "Ah hah! Come on! Yeah!" He was fired up and he in turn fired up the band. Paul Gonsalves closed his eyes and grimaced with intensity as he developed 27 consecutive spellbinding choruses. Jo Jones, Count Basie's former drummer, was the driving force behind Gonsalves and the Ellington orchestra that night. Duke later said, "If we had Count Basie at the piano and Freddie Green on guitar, we might have scorched the moon." After that night to remember, Duke made the front page of the Time magazine's next issue and he has since jokingly said he was born on July 8,1956, at Newport, Rhode Island.

"Duke Ellington was a genius, but his black skin prevented him from earning top dollar during his lifetime," Terry Clark says. "There was a limit on where and how he could work. You wouldn't believe it, man, but there was a time, when we played the Hotel Flamingo in Las Vegas, that Duke had to come through the kitchen in order to get to the bandstand, although his name was the top billing on the marquee. It was bigotry. It had a lot to do with the whole economic scene. They would not give this man an opportunity to put his music into proper perspective. They wouldn't let it reach the height it should have reached until after he was gone. He had to hustle and go out on the road and do one-nighters 365 days a year up until the end. He never had an opportunity to do a radio or television show like Benny Goodman or Tommy Dorsey.

"They kept him scuffling and batting his head against the wall. He was a courageous man because he refused to give up. He believed in his music and himself and he kept his band together until his legs wouldn't carry him anymore. Count Basie and Cab Calloway were also caught in that exploitation trap."

In 1959, Clark left Duke while on tour in Europe to join Quincy Jones in the Harold Arlen's blues opera "Free and Easy" Terry returned to New York in 1960 and became the first black staff musician for NBC. That job was a by-product of an Urban League affirmative action campaign against NBC for not employing more minorities. The staff band subsequently became the regular band on the Johnny Carson Tonight Show. It would be difficult for Terry to categorize that band because they had to swing, they played classical

Paul Gonsalves as he blows 27 consecutive spell binding choruses of "Diminuendo and Crescendo in Blue" at the Newport Jazz Festival on July 8,1956.

music, and in fact they had to play any kind of music that came along. It was a unique band, to say the least.

After Skitch Henderson left the show by special request, NBC received many letters asking that Clark Terry be made the bandleader. Management people at NBC thought that a black leader would affect their southern market, so they wouldn't give Clark the job. He also had the first shot at becoming the bandleader on the David Frost Show. But he turned that down because they wanted the band to play behind a screen out of sight of the television audience.

With the changing of the guard at NBC from Johnny Carson to Jay Leno, something strange happened. Leno made a dramatic switch from a white band leader to a black one in the person of Branford Marsalis. The southern market did not melt. As a matter of fact, in 1995 the Tonight Show was in a horse race with the CBS David Letterman Late Show. The two shows were running neck and neck.

Some people might say that Terry is picky. That may be true if getting a gig means he has to sacrifice his integrity. His television exposure has led to his ongoing involvement in education. Listeners wrote requests for different members of the Tonight Show band to appear at various high schools and colleges. An instrument company would sometimes sponsor these appearances and Clark Terry therefore has found himself involved on the music-clinic circuit full blast. It has given him an opportunity to stay involved with jazz education and he loves working with kids. This program gets Terry around to universities and colleges, high schools and grammar schools all over this country and in other parts of the world. Importantly, it keeps him involved with the perpetuation of his craft. It's refreshing to him and it keeps him on the ball. He knows that his craft is in good hands because young kids are getting into it.

The only thing that Terry finds disturbing is that the black kids are letting it slip through their fingers like sand. And it disturbs the hell out of him that black people are not interested in perpetuating jazz, their own original American art form-jazz.

Terry's considerable accomplishments as a jazz innovator and educator of the highest rank have earned an impressive array of awards. The University of New Hampshire, Berklee College of Music, and Teikyo Westmar University have bestowed honorary doctorates on Terry. Phi Mu Alpha Sinfonia national music fraternity made him the first jazz artist to be honored with its highest award for distinguished service to music. The U.S. Department of State selected Terry and his band for tours to the Middle East and Africa as American ambassadors of goodwill. He also was inducted into Kansas City's Jazz Hall of Fame.

Clark Terry discusses some of his concerns about black kids with Dempsey J. Travis.

Along with accepting honors, recordings and sell-out appearances at festivals and concerts, activities as a jazz educator have occupied Terry's attention. His dedication to the task of passing the torch of musical improvisation onto the next generation is second to none. Indeed, his rapport with students is summed up not only in great music but in the great smiles that the master and his students share in creating jazz as Ellington smiles down upon them from the big band in the sky.

Herb "Flamingo" Jeffries in 1941.

15 - HERB JEFFRIES: ELLINGTON'S FORGOTTEN FLAMINGO

In late October, 1994, I was enjoying a jazz cruise on board the S.S. Norway in the eastern Caribbean. It was on the Norway that I rediscovered Herb Jeffries, who was the surprise guest star appearing with the Duke Ellington Orchestra under the leadership of Mercer Ellington.

The Duke Ellington orchestra under the leadership of Mercer Ellington on the SS Norway in late October, 1994.

Seeing and hearing Herb sing several of my old favorites, including "Flamingo" and "Little Brown Book," was an unexpected, delightful treat. I had not seen him in person for more than 52 years. As a matter of fact, like most of his fans I thought he had made his final transition.

Writing a Duke Ellington book had been subliminally on my back burner for at least 30 years. During that period, I interviewed a number of the original Ellington men, including the Duke. Being captured at sea with Herb Jeffries was a great opportunity to get an interview and a different perspective from someone who had worked with the Duke during the second decade of his career.

During a relaxing moment between sets on the SS Norway, left to right, are Mercer Ellington, Dempsey J. Travis, and Paul, Mercer's son

During our talk, Herb Jeffries expressed some disappointment but did not express any bitterness because he had been treated as though he had not existed since 1942 when he was drafted into the Army during World War II. Jeffries showed some discomfort, saying, "When Stanley Dance wrote Duke's autobiography 'Music Is My Mistress,' I was not contacted to share my points of view about Ellington. As a matter of fact, not a single writer up to October 29, 1994, has interviewed me about the years I spent with his orchestra."

Jeffries recalled, "In 1985 there was a five-day jazz festival in England. Ellington's music was the central theme of the event. I was not invited, but I decided to go at my expense. A number of men who played with the Duke Ellington Orchestra during the 60's and 70's were on the program. Alice Babs from Sweden who worked in Ellington's sacred concerts was on the program and she sang several of Ellington's compositions.

"Yet I am the only person alive today who worked with the Duke in the late 1930's and early 40's. At age 83, I consider myself vintage Ellington. You cannot get any better than that," Herb Jeffries asserted.

Judging from Herb Jeffries's performances on the ship, I would say that he had never been better. His voice was strong, his delivery clear and he appeared to be as vigorous as an all-star football player. Black and white women on the ship went wild about his looks, his clothes and his ability to really belt out a song. He was their favorite until it was discovered that his "significant other" on the ship was a beautiful white girl who was

Herb Jeffries was never interviewed about his years with the Duke Ellington Orchestra.

at least 53 years his junior. This seeming turnaround did not phase blue-eyed Jeffries because he never considered skin color a barrier against falling in love.

Herb Jeffries attributes his taste in beautiful women and clothes to Duke Ellington. He said, "The Duke loved good food, lovely ladies and fine clothes. I have attempted to duplicate the Duke's flair for clothes. My closet is set up exactly like his. I still buy the same type of shoes that he wore. I wear my shirts, ties, suits and slacks in the same color combinations that he did. The pastel colors of his clothing were reflected in the various shades and moods of the music he composed. Unlike the music of the 70's, 80's and 90's, there is nothing violent in the Ellington song book. Even the orchestra's loud compositions like 'Rockin' In Rhythm' were lyrically passive.

Herb Jeffries is shown telling Dempsey J. Travis that he is the only person alive today who worked with Duke in the late 30's and early 40's.

Herb is shown singing "Little Brown Book" with the Ellington Orchestra on October 29, 1994.

"Ellington avoided everything that he perceived as being disruptive. He never fired anybody; he just made it inconvenient for them to work. If he had a misunderstanding with a woman he was living with, he simply left with just the clothes on his back, never to return for any of his personal belongings."

The well attired Duke Ellington that Herb Jeffries still remembers.

Jeffries recalled observing Duke on an airplane, "He did not like riding on planes or ships. On this particular trip I was sitting next to him watching him work. He was continually writing something and he must have felt my eyes staring at him.

"Duke looked up and asked, 'What is the matter Herbie?'

"I replied, 'Nothing.'

"Duke persisted, 'What's on your mind?'

"'I was just looking at you,' I said.

"'What are you thinking?' Duke asked.

"'I was just thinking it must be great to be up there,' was my reply.

"Duke sighed, 'Yes! It is great, but there is no place to sit down.'"

In the end we are all alone.

Wynton "The Jazz Torchbearer" Marsalis

EPILOGUE - WYNTON MARSALIS: THE JAZZ TORCHBEARER

When Louis Armstrong took his final intermission on July 7,1971, Wynton Marsalis was 9 years old. Duke Ellington joined "Satchmo" backstage on May 24, 1974, Wynton had not reached his 13th birthday. Yet Louis and Duke are mentors and heros to Marsalis.

Louis Armstrong in 1930

The first time I heard Wynton speak about the historical contributions of the two musical giants, Louis and Duke, he was 20 years old. He spoke with the seriousness and knowledge of a tenured professor, displaying a power of persuasion that would make a believer of anyone within the sound of his voice.

I met both of the jazz masters and many of their sidemen in the middle 1930's, yet never have I heard anyone Wynton's age speak of the giants of jazz with such conviction. Wynton talks with such personal identification about the masters, you feel that he was there. He is a master teacher and lecturer in the vein of Clark

Terry, another of his mentors. When Wynton was 15 years old, Terry sent him a postcard from Europe and Marsalis never forgot the thoughtfulness of that special touch.

Duke Ellington in 1933

If a person is not plastic, pictures on his or her walls give you some indication of how his head is screwed on and something about those individuals that he holds in high esteem. When you walk into Wynton Marsalis's midtown Manhattan apartment, you get a panoramic view of New York City, the Hudson River and portraits of Ellington, Armstrong and Art Blakey on the walls.

Wynton worships Louis Armstrong's style of playing, but his compositional work leans toward Ellington's suites and religious music. I attended all of Ellington's sacred concerts in San Francisco, New York City and Chicago, leaving all of them with a feeling of having been a part of an uplifting historical musical milestone.

On Wednesday, June 1,1994, I attended a three-hour religious concert entitled: "In This House, On This Morning," written by Wynton Marsalis and performed by his orchestra at the historic Quinn Chapel A. M. E. Church at 2401 South Wabash Avenue in Chicago. The event was billed as a religious concert, but in my opinion it was an old-time tent meeting revival. Every member of the band was an evangelist. If there was any room in your heart for God, the "Holy Ghost" gained entrance that evening.

The entire program was a deep religious experience and the audience became the eighth member of the band. The pew warmers' instruments were God-given: They used their feet, hands and voices. This was a concert that touched every nerve ending in the body.

I know that Duke Ellington and Louis Armstrong were smiling in approval of the young jazz torchbearer's performance as they watched from the wings.

Today jazz has reached a status that would have been considered a nightmare rather than a dream a decade ago. On December 18,1995, the Lincoln Center board elevated its jazz department to equal status with the New York Philharmonic, the Metropolitan Opera and the New York City Ballet. Carnegie Hall and Orchestra Hall in Chicago are moving in the same direction.

Lincoln Center's additional layer of respectability for America's original art form has to be attributed to Wynton Marsalis, the Jazz Torchbearer, and his Young Lions. Their commitment to the artistry of Armstrong, Duke, Eldridge, Dizzy, Parker, Blakey, Sarah, Ella, Basie, Jabbo, Mamie, Bessie, Webb, Lunceford, Henderson and Redman insures the lifespan of jazz until the end of time.

Wynton Marsalis, The Jazz Torchbearer and the Young Lions

COMPOSITIONS

Partial listing of Duke Ellington's compositions are listed here in their order of copyright.

Title of Composition	Year	Composer	Author
Blind Man's Bluff	1923	Duke Ellington	H. Trent
Choo Choo (I Gotta Hurry Home)	1924	Duke Ellington, Dave Ringle, and Bob Schaefer	
Pretty Soft For You	1924	Duke Ellington	Joseph Trent
Chocolate Kiddies:			
Jig Walk	1925	Duke Ellington	Jo Trent
Jim Dandy	1925	Duke Ellington	Jo Trent
With You	1925	Duke Ellington	Jo Trent
Yam Brown	1926	Duke Ellington	Jo Trent
The Blues I Love To Sing	1927	Duke Ellington and Bub Miley	
Black and Tan Fantasy	1927	Duke Ellington and Bub Miley	
East St. Louis Toodle-O	1927	Duke Ellington and Bub Miley	
Birmingham Breakdown (Breakdown)	1927	Duke Ellington	
Black Cat Blues	1927	Duke Ellington	
Hop Head	1927	Duke Ellington	
Immigration Blues	1927	Duke Ellington	
The Creeper	1927	Duke Ellington	
Washington Wabble	1927	Duke Ellington	
Down In Our Alley Blues	1927	Duke Ellington and Otto Hardwick	
Bouncing Buoyancy	1927	Duke Ellington	
Gold Digger	1927	Duke Ellington and Will Donaldson	
Hot and Bothered	1928	Duke Ellington	
Blue Bubbles	1928	Duke Ellington	
Creole Love Call	1928	Duke Ellington	
Black Beauty	1928	Duke Ellington	
Jubilee Stomp	1928	Duke Ellington	
New Orleans Low Down	1928	Duke Ellington	
Take It Easy	1928	Duke Ellington	
Swampy River	1928	Duke Ellington	

Title of Compostion	Year	Composer	Author
Move Over	1929	Duke Ellington	
Big House Blues	1929	Duke Ellington	
The Mooch	1929	Duke Ellington and Irving Mills	
Stevedore Stomp	1929	Duke Ellington and Irving Mills	
Harlem Flat Blues	1929	Duke Ellington	
Doin' the Voom Voom	1929	Duke Ellington	
Goin' to Town	1929	Duke Ellington and Bub Miley	
Flaming Youth	1929	Duke Ellington	
High Life	1929	Duke Ellington	
Memphis Wail	1929	Duke Ellington	
Mississippi Moan	1929	Duke Ellington	
Misty Mornin'	1929	Duke Ellington and Arthur Whetsol	
Rub-a-Tub-Lues	1929	Duke Ellington	
What a Life	1929	Duke Ellington	
Awful Sad	1929	Duke Ellington	
The Blues with a Feeling	1929	Duke Ellington	
Dicty Glide	1929	Duke Ellington	
The Duke Steps Out	1929	Duke Ellington	
Haunted Nights	1929	Duke Ellington	
Sloppy Joe	1929	Duke Ellington and Barney Bigard	
Rent Party Blues	1929	Duke Ellington and Johnny Hodges	
Saturday Night Function	1929	Duke Ellington and Albany Bigard	
Check and Double Check:			
Old Man Bites	1930	Duke Ellington	Duke Ellington and Irving Mills
Ring Dem Bells	1930	Duke Ellington	Duke Ellington and Irving Mills
The Breakfast Dance	1930	Duke Ellington	
Blues of the Vagabond	1930	Duke Ellington	
Cincinnati Daddy	1930	Duke Ellington	
Jazz Lips	1930	Duke Ellington	
The Lazy Duke	1930	Duke Ellington	
Syncopated Shuffle	1930	Duke Ellington	
Wall Street Wail	1930	Duke Ellington	
Sweet Mama	1930	Duke Ellington	
Zonky Blues	1930	Duke Ellington	
Blackberries of 1930:			

Title of Compostion	Year	Composer	Author
Bumpty Bump	1930	Duke Ellington	Irving Mills
Doin' the Crazy Walk	1930	Duke Ellington	Irving Mills
Swance River Rhapsody	1930	Duke Ellington, Irving Mills, and Clarence Gaskill	
I'm So in Love with You	1931	Duke Ellington and Irving Mills	
Rockin' Rhythm	1931	Duke Ellington, Irving Mills, and Harry Carney	
Mood Indigo	1931	Duke Ellington, Irving Mills, and Albany Bigard	
Rocky Mountain Blues	1932	Duke Ellington and Irving Mills	
Best Wishes	1932	Duke Ellington	Ted Koehler
Moon Over Dixie	1932	Duke Ellington	Ted Koehler
It Don't Mean a Thing If It Ani't Got That Swing	1932	Duke Ellington	Irving Mills
The Mystery Song	1932	Duke Ellington and Irving Mills	
Sweet Chariot	1932	Duke Ellington and Irving Mills	
Sophisticated Lady	1933	Duke Ellington	Mitchell Parish and Irving Mills
Drop Me Off in Harlem	1933	Duke Ellington	Nick Kenny
Slippery Horn	1933	Duke Ellington	
Jungle Nights in Harlem	1934	Duke Ellington and Irving Mills	
Dallas Doin's	1934	Duke Ellington	
Solitude	1934	Duke Ellington	Eddie De Lange and Irving Mills
Stompy Jones	1934	Duke Ellington	
Blue Feeling	1934	Duke Ellington	
Daybreak Express	1934	Duke Ellington	
Rude Interlude	1934	Duke Ellington	
Bird Of Paradise	1935	Duke Ellington	
Harlem Speaks	1935	Duke Ellington	
Delta Serenade	1935	Duke Ellington	Manny Kurtz and Irving Mills
In a Sentimental Mood	1935	Duke Ellington	Manny Kurtz and Irving Mills
Sump'n' 'Bout Rhythm	1935	Duke Ellington	Manny Kurtz and Irving Mills

Title of Compostion	Year	Composer	Author
Ducky Wucky	1935	Duke Ellington and Albany Bigard	
Hyde Park Merry Go Round	1935	Duke Ellington	
Reminiscing in Tempo	1935	Duke Ellington	
Showboat Schuffle	1935	Duke Ellington	
Saddest Tale	1935	Duke Ellington and Irving Mills	
Rhapsody Jr.	1935	Duke Ellington	
In a Jam	1936	Duke Ellington	
Clarinet Lament	1936	Duke Ellington and Barney Bigard	
Echoes of Harlem	1936	Duke Ellington	
Uptown Downboat	1936	Duke Ellington	
Trumpet in Spades	1936	Duke Ellington	
Yearning for Love	1936	Duke Ellington	Mitchell Parish and Irving Mills
Oh Baby, Maybe Someday	1936	Duke Ellington	Duke Ellington
Albany Home	1937	Duke Ellington and Dave Ringle	Duke Ellington and Dave Ringle
Caravan	1937	Duke Ellington and Juan Tizol	Irving Mills
Scattin' at the Kit Kat	1937	Duke Ellington	Irving Mills
Azure	1937	Duke Ellington	Irving Mills
Clouds in My Heart	1937	Duke Ellington and Barney Bigard	Irving Mills
Lament for Lost Love	1937	Duke Ellington and Barney Bigard	Irving Mills
Jazz a la Carte	1937	Duke Ellington and Barney Bigard	Irving Mills
Sauce for the Goose	1937	Duke Ellington and Barney Bigard	
Blue Reverie	1937	Duke Ellington and Harry Carney	
Demi-Tasse	1937	Duke Ellington and Harry Carney	
Ev'ah Day	1937	Duke Ellington and Harry Carney	
I've Got to Be a Rug Cutter	1937	Duke Ellington	Duke Ellington
Four and a Half Street	1937	Duke Ellington and Rex Stewart	
Black Butterfly	1937	Duke Ellington	Irving Mills and Ben Carruthers
Downtown Uproar	1937	Duke Ellington	

Title of Compostion	Year	Composer	Author
		and Cootie Williams	
Ridin' on a Blue Note	1938	Duke Ellington	Irving Mills and Irving Gordon
Jubilesta	1938	Duke Ellington and Juan Tizol	Irving Mills
Pyramid	1938	Duke Ellington and Juan Tizol	Irving Mills and Irving Gordon
Gypsy without a Song	1938	Duke Ellington and Lou Singer	Irving Gordon
Lost in Meditation	1938	Duke Ellington and Lou Singer	Irving Mills
Dusk on the Desert	1938	Duke Ellington	Irving Mills
Chasin' Chippies	1938	Duke Ellington and Cootie Williams	Irving Mills
Empty Ballroom Blues	1938	Duke Ellington and Cootie Williams	
Swing Pan Alley	1938	Duke Ellington and Cootie Williams	
Dinah's in a Jam	1938	Duke Ellington	
Swinging in the Dell	1938	Duke Ellington and Johnny Hodges	
Jeep's Blues	1938	Duke Ellington and Johnny Hodges	
Harmony in Harlem	1938	Duke Ellington and Johnny Hodges	Irving Mills
Jitterbug's Holiday	1938	Duke Ellington and Johnny Hodges	Irving Mills
Jeep Is Jumpin'	1938	Duke Ellington and Johnny Hodges	
Krum Elbow Blues	1938	Duke Ellington and Johnny Hodges	
Rhythmoods	1938	Duke Ellington	
Chatterbox	1938	Duke Ellington and Rex Stewart	Irving Mills
Steppin' Into Swing Society	1938	Duke Ellington	Irving Mills and Henry Nemo
I Let a Song Go Out of My Heart	1938	Duke Ellington	Irving Mills and John Redmond
Prelude to a Kiss	1938	Duke Ellington	Irving Mills and Irving Gordon
Drummer's Delight	1938	Duke Ellington and Barney Bigard	
Pigeons and Peppers	1938	Duke Ellington and Mercer Ellington	

Title of Compostion	Year	Composer	Author
La De Doody Doo	1938	Duke Ellington, Edward J. Lambert, and Stephen Richards	
Cotton Club Parade (4th ed.):			
I'm slappin' Seventh Avenue with the Sole of My Shoe	1938	Duke Ellington	Irving Mills and Henry Nemo
Skrontch	1938	Duke Ellington	Irving Mills and Henry Nemo
Swingtime in Honolulu	1938	Duke Ellington	Irving Mills and Henry Nemo
A Lesson In C	1938	Duke Ellington	Irving Mills and Henry Nemo
Braggin' in Brass	1938	Duke Ellington	Irving Mills and Henry Nemo
Carnival in Caroline	1938	Duke Ellington	Irving Mills and Henry Nemo
If You Were in My Place What Would You Do?	1938	Duke Ellington	Irving Mills and Henry Nemo
Battle of Swing	1939	Duke Ellington	
Blue Light	1939	Duke Ellington	
Boys from Harlem	1939	Duke Ellington	
The Buffet Flat	1939	Duke Ellington	
Delta Mood	1939	Duke Ellington	
Dooji Wooji	1939	Duke Ellington	
Exposition Swing	1939	Duke Ellington	
Gal from Joe's	1939	Duke Ellington	Irving Mills
I'm in Another World	1939	Duke Ellington and Johnny Hodges	Irving Mills and Irving Gordon
I'm Riding on the Moon and Dancing on the Stars	1939	Duke Ellington and Johnny Hodges	
Hodge Podge	1939	Duke Ellington and Johnny Hodges	
Wanderlust	1939	Duke Ellington and Johnny Hodges	
Subtle Lament	1939	Duke Ellington	
Hip Chic	1939	Duke Ellington	
Beautiful Romance	1939	Duke Ellington and Cootie Williams	Lupin Fein
Boudoir Benny	1939	Duke Ellington and Cootie Williams	
Gal-Avantin'	1939	Duke Ellington and Cootie Williams	

Title of Compostion	Year	Composer	Author
Mobile Blues	1939	Duke Ellington and Cootie Williams	
Jazz Potpourri	1939	Duke Ellington	
Boy Meets Horn	1939	Duke Ellington and Rex Stewart	Irving Mills
Smorgasbord and Schnapps	1939	Duke Ellington, Rex Stewart, and B. Fleagle	
Something to Live for	1939	Duke Ellington and Billy Strayhorn	Duke Ellington, Billy Strayhorn
Grievin'	1939	Duke Ellington and Billy Strayhorn	Duke Ellington, Billy Strayhorn
I'm Checking Out-Goom Bye	1939	Duke Ellington and Billy Strayhorn	Duke Ellington, Billy Strayhorn
Your Love Has Faded	1939	Duke Ellington and Billy Strayhorn	Duke Ellington, Billy Strayhorn
Lonely Co-ed	1939	Duke Ellington, B. Strayhorn, and Edgar Leslie	Duke Ellington, B. Strayhorn, and Edgae Leslie
Stevedore's Serenade	1939	Duke Ellington	Hilly Edelstein, Irving Gordon
You Gave Me the Gate and I'm Swinging	1939	Duke Ellington	I. Gordon, J. Farmer and J. B. McNeely
Watermelon Man	1939	Duke Ellington	Duke Ellington
Old King Dooji	1939	Duke Ellington	
Pussy Willow	1939	Duke Ellington	
Slap Happy	1939	Duke Ellington	
Solid Old Man	1939	Duke Ellington	
Way Low	1939	Duke Ellington	
Grateful to You	1939	Duke Ellington	
Lady in Doubt	1939	Duke Ellington	
Lady Macbeth	1939	Duke Ellington	
Lullaby	1939	Duke Ellington	
Country Gal	1939	Duke Ellington	
The Sargeant Was Shy	1939	Duke Ellington	
Tootin' Through the Roof	1939	Duke Ellington	
Weely	1939	Duke Ellington	
The Blues	1939	Duke Ellington	Irving Mills
Lady in Blue	1940	Duke Ellington	Irving Mills
Love's in My Heart	1940	Duke Ellington and Haynes Alvis	
Portrait of a Lion	1940	Duke Ellington	

Title of Compostion	Year	Composer	Author
Rumpus in Richmond	1940	Duke Ellington	
Sepia Panorama	1940	Duke Ellington	
Jack the Bear	1940	Duke Ellington	
Junior Hop	1940	Duke Ellington	
Pitter, Panther, Patter	1940	Duke Ellington	
Me and You	1940	Duke Ellington	Duke Ellington
Charlie the Chulo	1940	Duke Ellington	
Flaming Sword	1940	Duke Ellington	
My Sunday Gal	1940	Duke Ellington	
Diamond Jubilee Song	1940	Duke Ellington and Billy Strayhorn	Duke Ellington, Billy Strayhorn
Honchi Chonch	1940	Duke Ellington and Billy Strayhorn	Duke Ellington, Billy Strayhorn
Lick Chorus	1940	Duke Ellington	
Tonk	1940	Duke Ellington and Billy Strayhorn	
Day Dream	1940	Duke Ellington and Billy Strayhorn	John La Touche
A Lull at Dawn	1940	Duke Ellington	
Harlem Air Shaft	1940	Duke Ellington	
Conga Brava	1940	Duke Ellington and Juab Tizol	
A Portrait of Bert Williams	1940	Duke Ellington	
Bojangles	1940	Duke Ellington	
In a Mellow Tone (AKA: Baby, You and Me)	1940	Duke Ellington	Milt Gabler
I Never Felt This Way Before	1940	Duke Ellington	Al Dubin
All too Soon	1940	Duke Ellington	Carl Sigman
Concerto for Cootie (AKA: Cootie's Concerto)	1939	Duke Ellington	
Serenade to Sweden	1939	Duke Ellington	
Ko-Ko	1939	Duke Ellington	
Morning Glory	1939	Duke Ellington	
Blue Goose	1939	Duke Ellington	
Blue Bells of Harlem	1939	Duke Ellington	
Lovely Isle of Porto Rico (AKA: Porto Rico Gal)	1939	Duke Ellington and Juan Tizol	
Cotton Tail	1940	Duke Ellington	
Sapph	1940	Duke Ellington	
Slow Tune	1940	Duke Ellington	
Never No Lament	1940	Duke Ellington	
Flame Indigo	1941	Duke Ellington	Paul Webster
Doghouse Blues	1941	Duke Ellington	
Just A-Sittin' and A-Rockin'	1941	Duke Ellington and B. Strayhorn	Lee Gaines

Title of Compostion	Year	Composer	Author
Baby, When You Ain't There	1941	Duke Ellington	Mitchell Parish
I'm Satisfied	1941	Duke Ellington	Mitchell Parish
Swing Low	1941	Duke Ellington	
Lightin'			
Plucked Again	1941	Duke Ellington	
Swee' Pea	1941	Duke Ellington and B. Strayhorn	
Warm Valley	1941	Duke Ellington	Bob Russell
Rocks in My Bed	1941	Duke Ellington	Duke Ellington
Luna de Cuba (Spanish version of "Lovely Isle of Porto Rico)	1941	Duke Ellington and Juan Tizol	Sp.: George Negrette
Jump for Joy:			
I Got It Bad and That Ain't Good	1941	Duke Ellington	Paul Webster
Brown-Skin Gal in the Calico Gown	1941	Duke Ellington	Paul Webster
Chocolate Shake	1941	Duke Ellington	Paul Webster
Bessie-Whoa Babe	1941	Duke Ellington	Paul Webster
Nostalgia	1941	Duke Ellington	Paul Webster
Flame Indigo	1941	Duke Ellington	Paul Webster
Jump for Joy	1941	Duke Ellington	Paul Webster and Sid Kuller
Give Me an Old-Fashioned Waltz	1941	Duke Ellington	Sid Kuller
Sh, He's on the Beat	1941	Duke Ellington	Sid Kuller
Sharp Easter	1941	Duke Ellington	Sid Kuller
Bli-Blip	1941	Duke Ellington	Sid Kuller and Duke Ellington
The Giddy-Bug Galop	1941	Duke Ellington	
I Don't Know What Kind of Blues I Got	1942	Duke Ellington	Duke Ellington
Romance Wasn't Built in a Day	1942	Duke Ellington	
Fatstuff Serenade	1942	Duke Ellington and Rex Stewart	
Back Room Romp	1942	Duke Ellington and Rex Stewart	
San Juan Hill	1942	Duke Ellington, Rex Stewart, and B. Fleagle	
So, I'll Come Back for More	1942	Duke Ellington, Rex Stewart, and B. Fleagle	
Good Gal Blues	1942	Duke Ellington	
Bundle of Blues	1942	Duke Ellington	

Title of Compostion	Year	Composer	Author
Crescendo in Blue	1942	Duke Ellington	
Diminuendo in Blue	1942	Duke Ellington	
What Am I Here For?	1942	Duke Ellington	Frankie Laine
Azalea	1942	Duke Ellington	Duke Ellington
Going Up	1942	Duke Ellington	
I Don't Mind	1942	Duke Ellington	Billy Strayhorn
Someone	1942	Duke Ellington	
Little Posey	1942	Duke Ellington	
Don't Get Around Much Any More (vocal version of "Never No Lament")	1942	Duke Ellington	Bob Russell
Five O'Clock Drag	1942	Duke Ellington	Harold Adamson
Dusk	1942	Duke Ellington	
Oh, Miss Jaxson	1942	Duke Ellington	Duke Ellington
Sherman Shuffle	1942	Duke Ellington	
Are You Sticking?	1942	Duke Ellington	
Tea and Trumpets	1942	Duke Ellington	
C-Jam Blues (AKA: "C Blues")	1942	Duke Ellington	
American Lullaby (AKA: "Lullaby")	1942	Duke Ellington	
Home	1942	Duke Ellington	
Carnaval	1942	Duke Ellington and Juan Tizol	
Baby, Please Stop and Think About Me	1943	Duke Ellington	Irving Gordon
Tonight I Shall Sleep (with a Smile on My Face)	1943	Duke Ellington	Irving Gordon, Mercer Ellington
Mr. J. B. Blues	1943	Duke Ellington	
Mood to Be Wooed	1943	Duke Ellington and Johnny Hodges	
Killin' Myself	1943	Duke Ellington	
Grace Note Blues	1943	Duke Ellington	
Do Nothin' Till You Hear From Me (vocal version of "Concerto for Cootie")	1943	Duke Ellington	Bob Russell
Ring Around the Moon	1943	Duke Ellington	Bob Russell
Chicken Feed	1943	Duke Ellington	Bob Russell
Savoy Strut	1943	Duke Ellington and Johnny Hodges	
Rockabye River	1943	Duke Ellington	
Barzallai-Lou	1943	Duke Ellington	
Three Cent Stomp	1943	Duke Ellington	
Fickle Fling (AKA" Camp Grant Chant")	1943	Duke Ellington	
Graceful Awareness	1943	Duke Ellington	

Title of Compostion	Year	Composer	Author
Mobile Bay	1943	Duke Ellington and Rex Stewart	
Across the Track Blues	1943	Duke Ellington	
Blue Ramble	1943	Duke Ellington	Duke Ellington
Cotton Club Stomp	1943	Duke Ellington, Johnny Hodges, and Harry Carney	Duke Ellington, Johnny Hodges, Harry Carney
Shout 'Em, Aunt Tillie	1943	Duke Ellington and I. Mills	Duke Ellington and I. Mills
Main Stem (AKA: Altitude, Swing Shifters; Swing; On Becoming a Square)	1944	Duke Ellington	
Hit Me with a High Note and Watch Me Bounce	1944	Duke Ellington	Don George
I Didn't Know About You (vocal version of "Home")	1944	Duke Ellington	
I Ain't Got Nothin' but the Blues	1944	Duke Ellington	Don George
I'm Beginning to see the Light	1944	Duke Ellington , Don George, Johnny Hodegs, and Harry James	Duke Ellington, Don George, Johnny Hodges, and Harry James
Don't You Know I Care	1944	Duke Ellington	Mack David
No Smoking	1944	Duke Ellington	Duke Ellington
My Lovin' Baby and Me	1944	Duke Ellington , Don George, and Cab Calloway	Duke Ellington, Don George, and Cab Calloway
You Left Me Everything but You	1944	Duke Ellington and Don George	Duke Ellington and Don George
Jumping Frog Jump	1944	Duke Ellington	
Stomp, Look and Listen	1944	Duke Ellington	
Suddenly It Jumped	1944	Duke Ellington	
Jazz Convulsions	1944	Duke Ellington	
Creole Rhapsody	1944	Duke Ellington	Duke Ellington
I Can't Put My Arms Around a Memory	1944	Duke Ellington	Don George
Blutopia	1944	Duke Ellington	
You've Got My Heart (AKA: "Someone")	1944	Duke Ellington	
I Love My Lovin' Lover	1945	Duke Ellington	
Let the Zoomers Drool	1945	Duke Ellington and Johnny Hodges	
Esquire Swank	1945	Duke Ellington and Johnny Hodges	

Title of Compostion	Year	Composer	Author
The Wonder of You	1945	Duke Ellington and Johnny Hodges	Don George
Which Is Which Stomp	1945	Duke Ellington	
Heart of Harlem	1945	Duke Ellington	Langston Hughes
Fancy Dan	1945	Duke Ellington	
Riff'n Drill	1945	Duke Ellington	
Love, Strong and Consecutive	1945	Duke Ellington	Mack David
Subtle Slough	1945	Duke Ellington	
Zan	1945	Duke Ellington	
Unbooted Character	1945	Duke Ellington	
Bugle Breaks	1945	Duke Ellington, Billy Strayhorn, and Mercer Ellington	
Zanzibar	1945	Duke Ellington	
It's Only Account of You	1945	Duke Ellington	
Blue Cellophane	1945	Duke Ellington	
Air Conditioned Jungle	1945	Duke Ellington and Jimmy Hamilton	
Frustration	1945	Duke Ellington	
Strange Feeling	1945	Duke Ellington and Billy Strayhorn	
Coloratura	1945	Duke Ellington	
Dancers in Love (AKA: "Stomp for Beginners")	1945	Duke Ellington	
Prairie Fantasy	1945	Duke Ellington	
Downbeat Shuffle	1945	Duke Ellington	
Frantic Fantasy	1945	Duke Ellington and Rex Stewart	
Carnegie Blues	1945	Duke Ellington	
Teardrops in Rain	1945	Duke Ellington and William Anderson	
Ev'ry Hour on the Hour I Fall in Love with You	1945	Duke Ellington	Don George
Time's A-Wastin'	1945	Duke Ellington, Don George, and Mercer Ellington	
Everything but You	1945	Duke Ellington, Don George, and Harry James	
I'm just a Lucky So and So	1945	Duke Ellington	
New World A-Comin'	1945	Duke Ellington	
Translucency	1945	Duke Ellington	
Black, Brown and Beige: Emancipation Celebration	1945	Duke Ellington	

Title of Compostion	Year	Composer	Author
West Indian Dance	1945	Duke Ellington	
Sugar Hill Penthouse	1945	Duke Ellington	
Worksong	1945	Duke Ellington	
The Blues	1945	Duke Ellington	
Come Sunday	1945	Duke Ellington	
Metronome All Out	1945	Duke Ellington and Billy Strayhorn	
Suburbanite	1946	Duke Ellington	
Magenta Haze	1946	Duke Ellington	
Circe	1946	Duke Ellington	
Sono	1946	Duke Ellington	
Rugged Romeo	1946	Duke Ellington	
A Gatherin' in a Clearin'	1946	Duke Ellington and William Anderson	
Blue Abandon	1946	Duke Ellington	
Eight Veil	1946	Duke Ellington and Billy Strayhorn	
Fugue	1946	Duke Ellington	
Tic Toe Topic	1946	Duke Ellington and Oscar Pettiford	
Mellow Ditty	1946	Duke Ellington	
Hey, Baby	1946	Duke Ellington	
You Don't Love Me No More	1946	Duke Ellington	Duke Ellington
Pretty Woman	1946	Duke Ellington	Duke Ellington
Tonal Group:			
Rhapsoditti	1946	Duke Ellington	
Fugueaditti	1946	Duke Ellington	
Jam-a-ditty	1946	Duke Ellington	
Just Squeeze Me	1946	Duke Ellington	Lee Gaines
Tell Me, Tell Me, Dream Face	1946	Duke Ellington	Don George
It Shouldn't Happen to a Dream	1946	Duke Ellington and Johnny Hodges	Don George
You Gotta Crawl Before You Walk	1946	Duke Ellington, Larry Fotin, Mel Torme, And Robert Wells	Duke Ellington, Larry Fotin, Mel Torme, and Robert Wells
Deep South Suite:			
Happy Go Lucky Local	1947	Duke Ellington	
Sultry Sunset	1947	Duke Ellington	
Hearsay	1947	Duke Ellington and Billy Strayhorn	
There Was Nobody Looking	1947	Duke Ellington and Billy Strayhorn	
Magnolias Dripping with Honey	1947	Duke Ellington and Billy Strayhorn	

Title of Compostion	Year	Composer	Author
Golden Feather	1947	Duke Ellington and Al Sears	
He Makes Me Believe He's Mine	1947	Duke Ellington	John La Touche
It's Kind of Lonesome Out Tonight	1947	Duke Ellington	Don George
Indigo Echoes	1947	Duke Ellington and Irving Mills	Duke Ellington and Irving Mills
Tough Truckin'	1947	Duke Ellington and Irving Mills	Duke Ellington and Irving Mills
I Don't Know Why I Love You So	1947	Duke Ellington and Irving Mills	Duke Ellington and Irving Mills
T. T. on Toast	1947	Duke Ellington and Irving Mills	Duke Ellington and Irving Mills
You're Just an Old Antidisestab- lishmentarianismist	1947	Duke Ellington and Don George	Duke Ellington and Don George
Oh, Gee	1947	Duke Ellington	Duke Ellington
Boogie Bop Blue	1947	Duke Ellington	
Who Struck John? (AKA: "Blues")	1947	Duke Ellington and Johnny Hodges	
Frisky	1947	Duke Ellington and Johnny Hodges	
Far Away Blues	1947	Duke Ellington and Johnny Hodges	
Long Horn Blues	1947	Duke Ellington and Johnny Hodges	
Golden Cress	1947	Duke Ellington and Lawrence Brown	
Sultry Serenade	1947	Duke Ellington and Tyree Glenn	
The Beautiful Indians (Minnehaha)	1947	Duke Ellington	
The Beautiful Indians (Hiawatha)	1947	Duke Ellington and Al Sears	
Beggar's Hoilday	1947	Duke Ellington	
The Liberian Suite	1948	Duke Ellington	
Blues at Sundown	1952	Duke Ellington	Duke Ellington
A Tone Parallel to Harlem	1952	Duke Ellington	
Searsy's Blues	1952	Duke Ellington	
Personality	1952	Duke Ellington	
Blues for Blanton	1952	Duke Ellington	
Rock Skippin'	1952	Duke Ellington and Billy Strayhorn	

Title of Compostion	Year	Composer	Author
Smada	1952	Duke Ellington and Billy Strayhorn	
Come on Home	1952	Duke Ellington	Duke Ellington
Primping at the Prom	1953	Duke Ellington	
Merrie Mending	1953	Duke Ellington	Duke Ellington
Ballin' the Blues	1953	Duke Ellington	Duke Ellington
Satin Doll	1953	Duke Ellington	Billy Strayhorn, Johnny Mercer
Silver Cobwebs	1953	Duke Ellington	Don George
Nothin', Nothin', Baby (Without You)	1953	Duke Ellington	Duke Ellington
Kind of Moody (vocal version of "Serenade to Sweden"; AKA: "Moody")	1953	Duke Ellington	Carl Sigman
Chili Bowl	1954	Duke Ellington	
Who Knows	1954	Duke Ellington	
Janet	1954	Duke Ellington	
Reflections in D	1954	Duke Ellington	
One-Sided Love Affair	1954	Duke Ellington	
Serious Serenade in B-Flat Minor	1954	Duke Ellington	
Band Call	1954	Duke Ellington	
Alternate	1954	Duke Ellington	
Night Time	1954	Duke Ellington and Billy Strayhorn	Doris Julian
Tan Your Hide	1954	Duke Ellington and Billy Strayhorn	
Blossom	1954	Duke Ellington and Billy Strayhorn	John H. Mercer
What More Can I Say	1954	Duke Ellington	
Melancholia	1954	Duke Ellington	
Retrospection	1954	Duke Ellington	
B-Sharp Blues	1954	Duke Ellington	
My Reward	1955	Duke Ellington	
Night Creature (Parts 1-3)	1955	Duke Ellington	
Kinda Dukish	1955	Duke Ellington	
Reddy Eddy	1955	Duke Ellington	
It's Rumor	1955	Duke Ellington	Duke Ellington
Like a Train	1955	Duke Ellington	Duke Ellington
She	1955	Duke Ellington	Duke Ellington
Twilight Time	1955	Duke Ellington	Duke Ellington
Weatherman	1955	Duke Ellington	Duke Ellington
Hold Me Down Love	1955	Duke Ellington	Carl Sigman
Orson	1955	Duke Ellington	

Title of Compostion	Year	Composer	Author
		and Billy Strayhorn	
Oo	1955	Duke Ellington and Billy Strayhorn	Duke Ellington, Billy Strayhorn
Suburban Beauty	1956	Duke Ellingto	
Frivolous Banta	1956	Duke Ellington and Rick Henderson	
Cop-Out	1956	Duke Ellington	
Just Scratchin' the Surface	1956	Duke Ellington	
Rock 'n' Roll Rhapsody	1956	Duke Ellington	
Feetbone	1956	Duke Ellington	
Happy One	1956	Duke Ellington	
Killian's Lick	1956	Duke Ellington	
Coolin'	1956	Duke Ellington and Clark Terry	
Blue Rose	1956	Duke Ellington	
Lonesome Lullaby	1956	Duke Ellington	
Newport Jazz Festival Suite:			
Festival Junction	1956	Duke Ellington and Billy Strayhorn	
Newport Up	1956	Duke Ellington and Billy Strayhorn	
Blues to Be There	1956	Duke Ellington and Billy Strayhorn	
Big Drag	1956	Duke Ellington	
Falling Like a Raindrop	1956	Duke Ellington	
Clusterphobia	1956	Duke Ellington and Clark Terry	
The Sky Fell Down	1956	Duke Ellington	Joanne Towne
610 Suite	1956	Duke Ellington	
Scenic	1956	Duke Ellington	
A Drum Is a Woman:			
Ballet of the Flying Saucers	1956	Duke Ellington and Billy Strayhorn	
Congo Square	1956	Duke Ellington and Billy Strayhorn	
Carribee Joe	1956	Duke Ellington and Billy Strayhorn	
A Drum Is a Woman	1956	Duke Ellington and Billy Strayhorn	
Hey, Buddy Bolden	1956	Duke Ellington and Billy Strayhorn	
Madame Zaji	1956	Duke Ellington and Billy Strayhorn	
Rhumbob	1956	Duke Ellington and	

Title of Compostion	Year	Composer	Author
		Billy Strayhorn	
New Orleans	1956	Duke Ellington and	
		Billy Strayhorn	
Rhythm Pum Te Dum	1956	Duke Ellington and	
		Billy Strayhorn	
Zaji's Dream	1956	Duke Ellington and	
		Billy Strayhorn	
What Else Can You Do with a Drum?	1956	Duke Ellington and Billy Strayhorn	
Matumbe	1956	Duke Ellington and	
		Billy Strayhorn	
Finale	1956	Duke Ellington and	
		Billy Strayhorn	
Royal Ancestry (Portrait of Ella Fitzgerald):			
Beyond Category	1957	Duke Ellington and	
		Billy Strayhorn	
All Heart	1957	Duke Ellington and	
		Billy Strayhorn	
Total Jazz	1957	Duke Ellington and	
		Billy Strayhorn	
Shakespearean Suite:			
Half the Fun	1957	Duke Ellington and	
		Billy Strayhorn	
Madness in Great Ones	1957	Duke Ellington and	
		Billy Strayhorn	
Circle of Fourths	1957	Duke Ellington and	
		Billy Strayhorn	
Sonnet in Search of a Moor	1957	Duke Ellington and	
		Billy Strayhorn	
Lady Mac	1957	Duke Ellington and	
		Billy Strayhorn	
Sonnet to Hank Clinq	1957	Duke Ellington and	
		Billy Strayhorn	
Such Sweet Thunder	1957	Duke Ellington and	
		Billy Strayhorn	
Sonnet for Caesar	1957	Duke Ellington and	
		Billy Strayhorn	
The Telecasters	1957	Duke Ellington and	
		Billy Strayhorn	
Up and Down, Up and Down	1957	Duke Ellington and	
		Billy Strayhorn	
Star-Crossed Lovers	1957	Duke Ellington and	
		Billy Strayhorn	
Sonnet for Sister Kate	1957	Duke Ellington and	

Title of Compostion	Year	Composer	Author
		Billy Strayhorn	
Cafe Au Lait	1957	Duke Ellington	
Jumpy	1957	Duke Ellington and Rex Stewart	
Shades of Harlem	1957	Duke Ellington	
Wailing Interval	1957	Duke Ellington	
You Better Know It	1957	Duke Ellington	
Pomegranate	1957	Duke Ellington	Billy Strayhorn
Rock City Rock	1957	Duke Ellington	Duke Ellington
Love (My Everything)	1957	Duke Ellington	Duke Ellington
Duke's Place (vocal Version of "C-Jam Blues")	1957	Duke Ellington	Ruth roberts, Bill Katz, R. Thiele
Toot Suite:			
Red Shoes	1958	Duke Ellington and Billy Strayhorn	
Red Carpet	1958	Duke Ellington and Billy Strayhorn	
Red Garter	1958	Duke Ellington and Billy Strayhorn	
Ready-Go	1958	Duke Ellington and Billy Strayhorn	
Prima Bara Dubla	1958	Duke Ellington and Billy Strayhorn	
Jazz Festival Jazz	1958	Duke Ellington and Billy Strayhorn	
Blues in Orbit	1958	Duke Ellington and Billy Strayhorn	
Satin Doll	1958	Duke Ellington	Billy Strayhorn Johnny Mercer
Princess Blue	1958	Duke Ellington	
Controversial Suite:			
Before My Time	1958	Duke Ellington	
Later	1958	Duke Ellington	
Jones	1958	Duke Ellington and Pauline Reddon	
Pauline's Blues	1958	Duke Ellington and Pauline Reddon	
Pauline's Jump	1958	Duke Ellington and Pauline Reddon	
Blues in the Round	1958	Duke Ellington	
Hi Fi Fo Fum	1958	Duke Ellington	
Basement (AKA: "Trombone Trio")	1958	Duke Ellington	
Track 360 (AKA: "Trains That	1958	Duke Ellington	

Title of Compostion	Year	Composer	Author
Pass in the Night")			
Don't Ever Say Goodbye	1958	Duke Ellington, Bill Putnam, and Belinda Putnam	Duke Ellington, Bill Putman, and Belinda Putman
My Heart, My Mind, My Everything	1958	Duke Ellington	Duke Ellington
A Hundred Dreams from Now (AKA: "Champagne Oasis")	1958	Duke Ellington	Johnny Burke
E and D Blues	1958	Duke Ellington and John Sanders	
Pleadin'	1958	Duke Ellington	
Tune Poem	1958	Duke Ellington	
Soda Fountain Rag	1958	Duke Ellington	
Juniflip	1958	Duke Ellington	
Mr. Gentle and Mr. Cool	1958	Duke Ellington	
Jump for Joy:			
The Natives Are Restless Tonight	1959	Duke Ellington	Sid Kuller
Nerves, Nerves, Nerves	1959	Duke Ellington	Sid Kuller
Resigned to Living	1959	Duke Ellington	Sid Kuller
Strictly for Tourists	1959	Duke Ellington	Sid Kuller
Within Me I Know	1959	Duke Ellington	Sid Kuller
Three Shows for Clinkers	1959	Duke Ellington	Sid Kuller
Don't Believe Everything You Hear	1959	Duke Ellington	Sid Kuller
So the Good Book Says	1959	Duke Ellington and Billy Strayhorn	Sid Kuller
Walk It Off	1959	Duke Ellington and Billy Strayhorn	Sid Kuller
If We Were Anymore British (We Couln't Talk at all)	1959	Duke Ellington	Sid Kuller
Anatomy of a Murder (film score)	1959	Duke Ellington	
I'm Gonna Go Fishin' (theme from Anatomy of a Murder)	1959	Duke Ellington	Peggy Lee
Anatomy of a Murder:			
Flirtibird	1959	Duke Ellington	
Way Early Subtone	1959	Duke Ellington	
Hero to Zero	1959	Duke Ellington	
Low Key Lightly	1959	Duke Ellington	
Happy Anatomy	1959	Duke Ellington	
Midnight Indigo	1959	Duke Ellington	
Almost Cried	1959	Duke Ellington	
Sunswept Sunday	1959	Duke Ellington	

Title of Compostion	Year	Composer	Author
Grace Valse	1959	Duke Ellington	
Haupe	1959	Duke Ellington	
Upper and Outest	1959	Duke Ellington	
Do Not Disturb	1959	Duke Ellington	
Original	1959	Duke Ellington	
Bugs	1959	Duke Ellington	
Nymph	1959	Duke Ellington	
Tymperturbably Blue	1959	Duke Ellington and Billy Strayhorn	
Malleroba Spank	1959	Duke Ellington and Billy Strayhorn	
But	1959	Duke Ellington	Sid Kuller
When I Trilly with my Filly	1959	Duke Ellington	Sid Kuller
Show 'Em You Got Class	1959	Duke Ellington	Sid Kuller
Le Sucrier Velour	1959	Duke Ellington	
Lightning Bugs and Frogs	1959	Duke Ellington	
Walkin' and Singin' the Blues	1959	Duke Ellington	Lil Greenwood
Daul Fuel	1959	Duke Ellington and Clark Terry	
Launching Pad	1959	Duke Ellington and Clark Terry	
Idiom '59	1959	Duke Ellington	
Like Love (based on a theme from Anatomy of a Murder)	1960	Duke Ellington	Bob Russell
Cop-Out Extension	1959	Duke Ellington	
The Line-Up	1960	Duke Ellington and Paul Gonsalves	
Blues in Blueprint	1960	Duke Ellington	
The Swinger's Jump	1959	Duke Ellington	
Villes Ville Is the Place, Man	1960	Duke Ellington	
The Swingers Get the Blues Too	1960	Duke Ellington and Matthew Gee	
Idiom No. 2	1960	Duke Ellington	
Idiom No. 3	1960	Duke Ellington	
One More Once	1961	Duke Ellington	
The Beautiful Americans	1961	Duke Ellington	
I Want to Love You (theme from The Asphalt Jungle)	1961	Duke Ellington	Marshall Barer
Nutcracker Suite:			
Arabesque Cookie (Arabian Dance)	1960	Tchaikovsky, arr. Duke Ellington and Billy Strayhorn	
Dance of the Floreadores (Waltz of the Flowers)	1960	Tchaikovsky, arr. Duke Ellington and Billy Strayhorn	

Title of Compostion	Year	Composer	Author
Sugar Rum Cherry (Dance of the Sugar Plum Fairy)	1960	Tchaikovsky, arr. Duke Ellington and Billy Strayhorn	
Peanut Brittle Brigade (March)	1960	Tchaikovsky, arr. Duke Ellington and Billy Strayhorn	
Toot Toot Tootie Toot (Dance of the Reed Pipes)	1960	Tchaikovsky, arr. Duke Ellington and Billy Strayhorn	
Overture	1960	Tchaikovsky, arr. Duke Ellington and Billy Strayhorn	
Entr'acte	1960	Tchaikovsky, arr. Duke Ellington and Billy Strayhorn	
The Volga Vouty (Russian Dance)	1960	Tchaikovsky, arr. Duke Ellington and Billy Strayhorn	
Paris Blues:			
Battle Royal	1961	Duke Ellington	
Birdie Jungle	1961	Duke Ellington	
Autumnal Suite	1961	Duke Ellington	
Nite	1961	Duke Ellington	
Wild Man Moore	1961	Duke Ellington	
Paris Stairs	1961	Duke Ellington	
Guitar Amour	1961	Duke Ellington	
Paris Blues	1961	Duke Ellington	
Without a Word of Complaint	1961	Duke Ellington, Johnny Hodges, and George Weiss	Duke Ellington, Johnny Hodges, George Weiss
Starting With You (I'm Through)	1961	Duke Ellington, Johnny Hodges, and Pat Stewart	Duke Ellington, Johnny Hodges, and Pat Stewart
Sugar City (AKA: Pousse Cafe):			
Sugar City	1962	Duke Ellington	Marshall Barer
Spacious and Gracious	1962	Duke Ellington	Marshall Barer
Spider and Fly	1962	Duke Ellington	Marshall Barer
Settle for Less	1962	Duke Ellington	Marshall Barer
Swivel	1962	Duke Ellington	Marshall Barer
Forever	1962	Duke Ellington	Marshall Barer
Someone to Care For	1962	Duke Ellington	Marshall Barer
Je N'Ai Rien	1962	Duke Ellington	Marshall Barer

Title of Compostion	Year	Composer	Author
Here You Are	1962	Duke Ellington	Marshall Barer
Follow Me Up the Stairs	1962	Duke Ellington	Marshall Barer
Do Me a Favor	1962	Duke Ellington	Marshall Barer
These Are the Good Old Days	1962	Duke Ellington	Marshall Barer
Let's	1963	Duke Ellington	Marshall Barer
Amazing	1963	Duke Ellington	Marshall Barer
The Colonel's Lady	1963	Duke Ellington	Marshall Barer
Natchez Trace	1964	Duke Ellington	Marshall Barer
Goodbye, Charlie	1964	Duke Ellington	Marshall Barer
Thank Yo, Sam	1964	Duke Ellington	Marshall Barer
C'est Comme Ca	1964	Duke Ellington	Marshall Barer
And Then Some	1962	Duke Ellington	Johnny Hodges
Suite Thursday:			
Lay Be	1962	Duke Ellington	
Misfit Blues	1962	Duke Ellington	
Zweet Zurzday	1962	Duke Ellington	
Schwiphti	1962	Duke Ellington	
Peer Gynt Suite	1962	Grieg, arr. Duke Ellington and Billy Strayhorn	
Tell Me	1962	Duke Ellington and Matthew Gee, Jr.	
Lazy Rhapsody	1962	Duke Ellington	Mitchell Parish
Argentine	1962	Duke Ellington	Mitchell Parish
Blue Mood	1962	Duke Ellington and Johnny Hodges	Duke Ellington, Johnny Hodges
Dear	1962	Duke Ellington and Donald Heywood	
Framed	1962	Duke Ellington and Donald Heywood	Andy Razaf
Down Home Stomp	1962	Duke Ellington	Jo Trent
Fast and Furious	1962	Duke Ellington and Harold Pottio	
Glamorous	1962	Duke Ellington	Jo Trent and Irving Mills
Jollywog	1962	Duke Ellington	
Keep on Treating Me Sweet	1962	Duke Ellington	Jo Trent
Lot O' Fingers	1962	Duke Ellington	
A Night in Harlem	1962	Duke Ellington	
Oklahoma Stomp	1962	Duke Ellington	
Savage Rhythm	1962	Duke Ellington	
Slow Motion	1962	Duke Ellington	
Sponge Cake and Spinach	1962	Duke Ellington	
Swanee Lullaby	1962	Duke Ellington, Mitchell Parish,	Duke Ellington, Mitchell Parish,

Title of Compostion	Year	Composer	Author
		and Irving Mills	and Irving Mills
Sweet Dreams of Love	1962	Duke Ellington and Irving Mills	
What Would It Mean Without You?	1962	Duke Ellington, Irving Mills, and George Brown	
Who Is She?	1962	Duke Ellington, Rousseau Simmons, Irving Mills, and Bob Schafer	Duke Ellington, Rousseau Simmons, Irving Mills, and Bob Schafer
Who Said It's Tight Like This?	1962	Duke Ellington	
Wring Your Washin' Out	1962	Duke Ellington and Jo Trent	
Introspection	1962	Duke Ellington	
Reconversion	1962	Duke Ellington	
The Feeling of Jazz	1962	Duke Ellington	Bobby Troup and George T. Simon
Twistin' Time	1962	Duke Ellington	Aaron Bell
Jump Over	1962	Duke Ellington	
Single Petal of a Rose	1962	Duke Ellington	
B.D.B	1962	Duke Ellington and Billy Strayhorn	
Self-Portrait of the Bean	1962	Duke Ellington and Billy Strayhorn	
Stand By Blues	1962	Duke Ellington	Johnny Hodges
You've Got The Love I Love	1962	Duke Ellington and Della Reese	Duke Ellington and Della Reese
Limbo Jazz	1962	Duke Ellington	
Java Pachacha	1962	arr. Duke Ellington	
Caline	1963	Duke Ellington	
Volupte	1963	Duke Ellington	
Purple Gazelle (Angelica)	1963	Duke Ellington	
Angu	1963	Duke Ellington	
Bonga	1963	Duke Ellington	
Moon Bow	1963	Duke Ellington	
Afro-Bossa	1963	Duke Ellington	
Fleurette Africaine	1963	Duke Ellington	
Wig Wise	1963	Duke Ellington	
Very Special	1963	Duke Ellington	
The Ricitic	1963	Duke Ellington	
Take the Coltrane	1963	Duke Ellington	
Money Jungle	1963	Duke Ellington	
You Dirty Dog	1963	Duke Ellington	
Ain't But the One	1963	Duke Ellington	
Will You Be There?	1963	Duke Ellington	

Title of Compostion	Year	Composer	Author
Heritage	1963	Duke Ellington	
Ninety-Nine Per Cent	1963	Duke Ellington	
King Fit the Battle of Alabam	1963	Duke Ellington	Duke Ellington
Blow by Blow	1963	Duke Ellington	
The Good Years of Jazz	1963	Duke Ellington	
Silk Lace	1963	Duke Ellington	
Sempre Amore	1963	Duke Ellington	
Blue Piano	1963	Duke Ellington	Ruth Roberts, Bill Katz, and Bob Thiele
Action in Alexandria	1963	Duke Ellington	
Ray Charle's Place	1963	Duke Ellington	
Perfume Suite:	1963	Duke Ellington	
Strange Feeling	1963	Duke Ellington	
Balcony Serenade	1963	Duke Ellington	
Coloratura	1963	Duke Ellington	
Dancers in Love	1963	Duke Ellington	
Ever-Lovin' Lover	1963	Duke Ellington	Duke Ellington
What Color Is Virtue?	1963	Duke Ellington	Duke Ellington
After Bird Jungle	1963	Duke Ellington	
Jail Blues	1963	Duke Ellington	
Jungle Triangle	1963	Duke Ellington	
Blues for Jerry (AKA: "Blues to Jerry")	1963	Duke Ellington	
A Hundred Dreams Ago	1963	Duke Ellington	
Fountainbleau Forest	1963	Duke Ellington	
So	1963	Duke Ellington	
It's Bad to Be Forgotten	1963	Duke Ellington	
Congo	1963	Duke Ellington	
Springtime in Africa	1964	Duke Ellington and Aaron Bell	
M.G.	1964	Duke Ellington	
La Scala, She Too Pretty to Be True	1964	Duke Ellington	
Non-Violent Integration	1964	Duke Ellington	
Timon of Athens Suite:			
Impulsive Giving	1964	Duke Ellington	
Ocean	1964	Duke Ellington	
Angry	1964	Duke Ellington	
Gold	1964	Duke Ellington	
Regal Formal	1964	Duke Ellington	
Regal	1964	Duke Ellington	
Skilipop	1964	Duke Ellington	
Smoldering	1964	Duke Ellington	
Gossippippi	1964	Duke Ellington	

Title of Compostion	Year	Composer	Author
Counter Theme	1964	Duke Ellington	
Alcibiades	1964	Duke Ellington	
Gossip	1964	Duke Ellington	
Banquet	1964	Duke Ellington	
Revolutionary	1964	Duke Ellington	
The Far East Suite:			
Blue Bird of Delhi	1964	Duke Ellington and Billy Strayhorn	
Vict	1964	Duke Ellington and Billy Strayhorn	
Depk	1964	Duke Ellington and Billy Strayhorn	
Elf (Isfahan)	1964	Duke Ellington and Billy Strayhorn	
Circle	1964	Duke Ellington and Billy Strayhorn	
Agra	1964	Duke Ellington and Billy Strayhorn	
Paki	1964	Duke Ellington and Billy Strayhorn	
Amad	1964	Duke Ellington and Billy Strayhorn	
Put-Tin	1964	Duke Ellington and Billy Strayhorn	
Blue Pepper	1964	Duke Ellington and Billy Strayhorn	
Tourist Point of View	1964	Duke Ellington and Billy Strayhorn	
Sex, Money nd Marriage	1964	Duke Ellington	
Tuttie for Cootie	1964	Duke Ellington	Jimmy Hamilton
Searchin'	1964	Duke Ellington	Steve Allen
Workin' Blues	1964	Duke Ellington	
My Man Sends Me	1964	Duke Ellington	Duke Ellington
My Mother, My Father and Love	1964	Duke Ellington	Duke Ellington
Metromedia	1964	Duke Ellington	
Stoona	1964	Duke Ellington	
New Tootie for Cootie	1964	Duke Ellington	
Rude Interlude	1964	Duke Ellington	
It's Glory	1964	Duke Ellington	
Warm Fire	1965	Duke Ellington	
Making That Scene	1965	Duke Ellington	Duke Ellington
58th Street Suite	1965	Duke Ellington and Billy Strayhorn	

Title of Compostion	Year	Composer		Author
Ellington '66	1965	Duke Ellington		
The Far East Suite:				
Fugi	1965	Duke Ellington		
Ad Lib on Nippon	1965	Duke Ellington		
Nagoya	1965	Duke Ellington		
Love Came	1965	Billy Strayhorn		Duke Ellington
The Truth	1965	Duke Ellington		Duke Ellington
On Account of You	1965	Duke Ellington		
Concerto for Oscar	1965	Duke Ellington		
Be a Man	1965	Duke Ellington		Marshall Barer
Flugal Street Rag	1965	Duke Ellington		Marshall Barer
My Heart Is a Stranger	1965	Duke Ellington		Marshall Barer
Rules and Regulations	1965	Duke Ellington		Marshall Barer
Salvation	1965	Duke Ellington		Marshall Barer
Up Your Ante	1965	Duke Ellington		Marshall Barer
A Girl's Best Friend	1965	Duke Ellington		Marshall Barer
The Golden Broom and the Green Apple	1965	Duke Ellington		Marshall Barer
Virginia Island Suite:				
Fiddler on the Diddler	1965	Duke Ellington Billy Strayhorn	and	
Island Virgin	1965	Duke Ellington Billy Strayhorn	and	
Virgin Jungle	1965	Duke Ellington Billy Strayhorn	and	
Jungle Kitty	1965	Duke Ellington Billy Strayhorn	and	
Big Fat Alice's Blues	1965	Duke Ellington Billy Strayhorn	and	
Mysterious Chick	1965	Duke Ellington Billy Strayhorn	and	
Fade Up	1965	Duke Ellington Billy Strayhorn	and	
Barefoot Stomper	1965	Duke Ellington Billy Strayhorn	and	
Tokyo	1965	Duke Ellington Jim Hamilton	and	
In the Beginning God (Pacabe) (Olds)	1965	Duke Ellington		
The Lord's Prayer	1965	Duke Ellington		
Christmas Surprise	1965	Duke Ellington	and	Rev. D. J. Bartlett
Thank You Ma'am (from "Pousse Cafe")	1966	Duke Ellington		
Spanking Brand New Doll	1966	Duke Ellington		Duke Ellington

Title of Compostion	Year	Composer	Author
Imagine My Frustration	1966	Duke Ellington, Billy Strayhorn, and Gerald Wilson	Duke Ellington, Billy Strayhorn, and Gerald Wilson
Imbo (Limbo Jazz)	1966	Duke Ellington	
Tell Me It's the Truth	1966	Duke Ellington	Duke Ellington
House of Lords (l'Earl, le Duke)	1966	Earl Hines and Duke Ellington	Earl Hines and Duke Ellington
The Second Portrait of the Lion	1966	Duke Ellington	Duke Ellington
Jive Stomp	1966	Duke Ellington	Duke Ellington
Mount Harissa	1966	Duke Ellington	Duke Ellington
The Twitch	1966	Duke Ellington	
A Song for Christmas	1966	Dean Bartlett, Duke Ellington, and Billy Strayhorn	Dean Bartlett, Duke Ellington, Billy Strayhorn
You Walk in My Dreams	1966	Duke Ellington	
You Are Beautiful	1966	Duke Ellington	
West Indian Pancake	1966	Duke Ellington	
Veldt-Amor	1966	Duke Ellington	
The Twitch	1966	Duke Ellington	
Three	1967	Duke Ellington	
This Man	1967	Duke Ellington	
Plaything	1967	Duke Ellington	
New Shoes	1967	Duke Ellington	
Nob Hill	1967	Duke Ellington	
My Home Lies Quiet	1967	Duke Ellington	
To the Better	1967	Duke Ellington	
Tin Soldier	1967	Duke Ellington	
They Say	1967	Duke Ellington	
Man Sees Nothing	1967	Duke Ellington	
The Man Beneath	1967	Duke Ellington	
Malay Camp	1967	Duke Ellington	
La Plus Belle Africaine:			
Laying on Mellow	1967	Duke Ellington	
Kisse	1967	Duke Ellington	
J. P. Williamson	1967	Duke Ellington	
I Like Singing	1967	Duke Ellington	
Full of Shadows	1967	Duke Ellington	
Eliza	1967	Duke Ellington	
Crispy	1967	Duke Ellington	
Come Easter	1967	Duke Ellington	
Circus	1967	Duke Ellington	
Cham	1967	Duke Ellington	
Canon	1967	Duke Ellington	

Title of Compostion	Year	Composer	Author
Fatness	1967	Duke Ellington	
Baby, You're Too Much	1967	Duke Ellington and Don George	Duke Ellington and Don George
The Matador (El Viti)	1967	Duke Ellington	
Poco Mucho	1967	Duke Ellington	
Workin' Blues	1967	Duke Ellington	
Salute to Morgan State	1967	Duke Ellington	
Rock the Clock	1967	Duke Ellington	
Ocht O' Clock Rock	1967	Duke Ellington	
Where in the World?	1967	Duke Ellington	
Rue Bleue	1967	Duke Ellington	
Up Jump	1967	Duke Ellington	
Swamp Goo	1967	Duke Ellington	
Rondelet	1967	Duke Ellington	
Mara-Gold	1967	Duke Ellington	
Lele	1967	Duke Ellington	
Lady	1967	Duke Ellington	
Bolling	1967	Duke Ellington	
Chromatic Love Affair	1967	Duke Ellington	
Drag	1967	Duke Ellington	
Eggo	1967	Duke Ellington	
Girdle Hurdle	1967	Duke Ellington	
Traffic Jam	1967	Duke Ellington	
Murder in the Cathedral:			
Becket	1967	Duke Ellington	
Gold	1967	Duke Ellington	
Land	1967	Duke Ellington	
Martyr	1967	Duke Ellington	
Women's	1967	Duke Ellington	
Exotique Bongos	1967	Duke Ellington	
The Second Sacred Concert:			
The Biggest and Busiest Intersection	1968	Duke Ellington	
The Shepherd	1968	Duke Ellington	
Meditation	1968	Duke Ellington	
Father Forgive	1968	Duke Ellington	Duke Ellington
Don't Get Down on Your Knees to Pray Until You Have Forgiven Everyone	1968	Duke Ellington	Duke Ellington
God Has Those Angels	1968	Duke Ellington	Duke Ellington
Heaven	1968	Duke Ellington	Duke Ellington
T.G.T.T.	1968	Duke Ellington	Duke Ellington
Something 'Bout Believing	1968	Duke Ellington	Duke Ellington
Freedom (parts 1-7)	1968	Duke Ellington	Duke Ellington
Freedom (Word You Heard)	1968	Duke Ellington	Duke Ellington

Title of Compostion	Year	Composer	Author
Freedom (Sweet Fat and That)	1968	Duke Ellington and Willie Smith	Duke Ellington and Willie Smith
Praise God and Dance	1968	Duke Ellington	
Finesse	1968	Duke Ellington and Johnny Hodges	Duke Ellington, Johnny Hodges
Night Train to Memphis	1968	Duke Ellington and Cat Anderson	Duke Ellington and Cat Anderson
Tokyo (from "Ad Lib on Nippon")	1968	Duke Ellington and Jimmy Hamilton	Duke Ellington, Jimmy Hamilton
Be Cool and Groovy for Me	1968	Duke Ellington, Cootie Williams, and Tony Bennett	Duke Ellington, Cootie Williams, and Tony Bennett
Keor	1968	Duke Ellington	
Kiki	1968	Duke Ellington	
Ritz	1968	Duke Ellington	
I Fell and Broke My Heart	1968	Duke Ellington	Don George
You're a Little Black Sheep	1968	Duke Ellington	Don George
You Make That Hat Look Pretty	1968	Duke Ellington	Duke Ellington
Woman	1968	Duke Ellington	Duke Ellington
I Have Given My Love Petremont	1968	Duke Ellington	Patricia
When You've Had It All Petremont	1968	Duke Ellington	Patricia
My Lonely Love Petremont	1968	Duke Ellington	Patricia
Knuf	1969	Duke Ellington	
Reva	1969	Duke Ellington	
Elos	1969	Duke Ellington	
Gigl	1969	Duke Ellington	
Moon Maiden	1969	Duke Ellington	Duke Ellington
The Moon Suite	1969	Duke Ellington	Duke Ellington
Anticipation and Hesitation	1969	Duke Ellington	Duke Ellington
Just a Gentle Word from You and	1969	Duke Ellington and	Duke Ellington
Will Do		Onzy Matthews	Onzy Matthews
Mexicali Brass	1969	Duke Ellington and Onzy Matthews	Duke Ellington, Onzy Matthews
Fifi	1970	Duke Ellington	
Pamp	1970	Duke Ellington	
Rapid	1970	Duke Ellington	
The Spring	1970	Duke Ellington	

Title of Compostion	Year	Composer	Author
Opus 69	1971	Duke Ellington	
Cafe	1971	Duke Ellington	Duke Ellington
The Blues Ain't	1971	Duke Ellington	Duke Ellington
99 Percent	1971	Duke Ellington	Duke Ellington
Lovin' Lover	1971	Duke Ellington	Duke Ellington
Perdido Cha Cha Cha Cha	1971	Duke Ellington	Duke Ellington
New Orleans Suite:			
Bourbon Street Jingling Jollies	1971	Duke Ellington	
Aristocracy a la Jean Lafitte	1971	Duke Ellington	
Thanks for the Beautiful Land on the Delta	1971	Duke Ellington	
Blues for New Orleans	1971	Duke Ellington	
Second Line	1971	Duke Ellington	
Portrait of Wellman Braud	1971	Duke Ellington	
Portrait of Louis Armstrong	1971	Duke Ellington	
Portrait of Mahalia Jackson	1971	Duke Ellington	
Portarit of Sidney Bechet	1971	Duke Ellington	
Brot	1971	Duke Ellington	
Snek	1971	Duke Ellington	
Roth	1971	Duke Ellington	
Math	1971	Duke Ellington	
Loud	1971	Duke Ellington	
The Hard Way	1971	Duke Ellington	
Black Swan	1970	Duke Ellington	
Fife	1970	Duke Ellington	
4:30 Blues	1970	Duke Ellington	
Hard	1970	Duke Ellington	
In Triplicate	1970	Duke Ellington	
Mixt	1970	Duke Ellington	
What Time Is It?	1970	Duke Ellington	
Soft	1970	Duke Ellington	
Afrique	1970	Duke Ellington	
Rext	1970	Duke Ellington	
Stud	1970	Duke Ellington	
The River:			
Well	1970	Duke Ellington	
Run	1970	Duke Ellington	
The Giggling Rapids	1970	Duke Ellington	
Meander	1970	Duke Ellington	
The Lake	1970	Duke Ellington	
The Falls	1970	Duke Ellington	
The Whirlpool	1970	Duke Ellington	
The River	1970	Duke Ellington	

Title of Compostion	Year	Composer	Author
The Village of the Virgins	1970	Duke Ellington	
The Mother, Her Majesty the Sea	1970	Duke Ellington	
Hick	1971	Duke Ellington	
Dick	1971	Duke Ellington	
Road of the Phoebe Snow	1971	Duke Ellington and Billy Strayhorn	Duke Ellington, Billy Strayhorn
Everybody Wants to Know Why I Sing the Blues	1971	Duke Ellington	
Afro-Eurasian Eclipse:			
Dash	1971	Duke Ellington	
Buss	1971	Duke Ellington	
Acac	1971	Duke Ellington	
Yoyo	1971	Duke Ellington	
True	1971	Duke Ellington	
Tenz	1971	Duke Ellington	
Tego	1971	Duke Ellington	
Soso	1971	Duke Ellington	
Nbdy	1971	Duke Ellington	
Gong	1971	Duke Ellington	
Dijb	1971	Duke Ellington	
Sche	1971	Duke Ellington	
The Goutelas Suite:			
Goof	1971	Duke Ellington	
Gogo II	1971	Duke Ellington	
Gogo I	1971	Duke Ellington	
Gigi	1971	Duke Ellington	
Ray Charles' Place	1971	Duke Ellington	
Tina	1972	Duke Ellington	Duke Ellington
Everyone	1972	Duke Ellington	Duke Ellington
Almighty God	1972	Duke Ellington	Duke Ellington
Mich	1972	Duke Ellington	
New York, New York	1972	Duke Ellington	Duke Ellington
Rainy Nights	1973	Duke Ellington	Duke Ellington
Jumping Room Only	1973	Duke Ellington	Duke Ellington
Celebration	1973	Duke Ellington	Duke Ellington
Soul Flute (Flute Ame)	1973	Duke Ellington	
Addi	1973	Duke Ellington	
Togo Brava Suite:			
Right On Togo	1973	Duke Ellington	
Soul Soothing Beach	1973	Duke Ellington	
Naturelement	1973	Duke Ellington	
Amour, Amour	1973	Duke Ellington	

BIBLIOGRAPHY

INTERVIEWS (Taped one-on-one with the author. Most of the interviews were later supplemented by one or more telephone calls.)

Lil Armstrong, June 16,1970.
   Occupation: Bandleader, Arranger and Composer
   Instrument Played: Piano
   Played With: King Oliver, Freddie Keppard and her husband, Louis Armstrong.

Etta Moten Barnett, May 6,1992.
   Occupation: Broadway and Hollywood Singing Star
   She appeared on Broadway in "Porgy and Bess" and the Hollywood movie "Golddiggers of 1933" singing "Remember My Forgotten Man." She also sang the "Carioca" in the picture "Flying Down to Rio" (1934).

Louie Bellson, June 31,1983.
   Occupation: Bandleader, Arranger and Composer
   Instrument Played: Drums
   Played With: Tommy Dorsey, Harry James and Duke Ellington.

Ken Blewett, April 7, 1982.
   Occupation: Manager of the Regal, Roosevelt and Tivoli Theaters

Johnny Board
   Occupation: Bandleader, Composer and Arranger
   Instruments Played: Tenor and Alto Saxophone
   Played With: Count Basie, Coleman Hawkins, Woody Herman, Red Saunders, Johnny Long, B. B. King, Jesse Miller, Bobby Blue Bland and Ruth Brown.

Roy Butler, March 16, 1982.
Instrument Played: Reeds
Played With: Sammy Stewart, Leon Abbey, Jimmy Wade, Harry
Fleming in Europe, Herb Fleming in Europe and South America,
Teddy Weatherford in the U.S.A..

Cab Calloway, January 14, 1983.
Occupation: Bandleader, Vocalist, Broadway and Hollywood Actor,
Dancer and Drummer.
Played With: Louis Armstrong, Blanche Calloway (his sister),
Alabamians and the Missourians.

Floyd Campbell, April, 1982.
Occupation: Bandleader
Instrument Played: Drums
Played With: Jabbo Smith, Louis Armstrong, Charlie Creath, Fate
Marable and Al Trent.

Carol Chilton
Occupation: Dancer, Singer, Pianist and Composer
Instrument Played: Piano
Played With: Al Jolson, Kate Smith, Eddie Cantor, Jimmy Durante,
Duke Ellington, Don Redman, Noble Sissle, The Whitman Sisters,
Mills Brothers, Bill Robinson, Milton Berle, Mae West, George Burns,
Gracie Allen and Eubie Blake.

Oliver Coleman, February, 1961.
Instrument Played: Drums
Played With: Ray Nance, Earl Hines, Erskine Tate and Horace
Henderson.

Holmes "Daddy-O" Daylie, September 18,1982.
Occupation: Radio and Television Personality

Barrett Deems, October, 1982.
Occupation: Bandleader and Sideman
Instrument Played: Drums
Played With: Paul Ash, Joe Venuti, Jimmy Dorsey, Tommy Dorsey,

Charlie Barnet, Woody Herman, Red Norvo, Muggsy Spanier, Louis Armstrong, Jack Teagarden and The Dukes of Dixieland.

George Dixon, April 21, 1982.
Occupation: Instrumentalist and Bandleader
Instruments Played: Violin, Trumpet and Saxophone
Played With: Sammy Stewart, Earl Hines, Floyd Campbell and Eddie King.

Dorothy Donegan, June, 1983.
Occupation: Jazz Artist
Instrument Played: Piano
Featured In: Movies, Television, Nightclubs, Broadway Plays and Concert Halls throughout America and Europe.

Billy Eckstine, July 7, 1983.
Occupation: Vocalist, Songwriter and Bandleader
Instruments Played: Trumpet, Valve Trombone and Guitar
Played With: Tommy Myles and Earl Hines.

Mercer Ellington, October 29,1994.
Occupation: Composer and Bandleader
Instrument Played: Trumpet
Played With: His father Duke Ellington.

Marty Faye, February 24, 1983.
Occupation: Radio Disc Jockey and Television Personality.

Henry Fort, February 16, 1983.
Instrument Played: Bass Fiddle
Played With: Nat "King" Cole and others.

Bud Freeman, October 12,1983.
Occupation: Tenor Saxophonist, Composer and Bandleader
Instruments Played: Tenor Saxophone and Clarinet
Played With: Husk O'Hare Wolverines, Ben Pollack, Red Nichols, Meyer Davis, Tommy Dorsey, Benny Goodman and Eddie Condon.

Dizzy Gillespie, June 2, 1982.
Occupation: Instrumentalist, Composer, Vocalist and Bandleader
Instrument Played: Trumpet
Played With: Cab Calloway, Lucky Millinder, Charlie Barnet, Fletcher Henderson, Benny Carter, Earl Hines, Duke Ellington, John Kirby and Billy Eckstine.

Harry Gray [President of Local 208, affiliate of the American Federation of Musicians], October, 1982.

Sonny Greer, July 14,1969.
Occupation: Drummer
Played With: Duke Ellington for 31 years.

Johnny Griffin
Occupation: Bandleader, Composer and Arranger
Instruments Played: Tenor Saxophone and Clarinet
Played With: Lionel Hampton, The Jazz Messengers, Thelonious Monk, Gene Ammons, Lester Young, Walter Dyett, T-Bone Walker and Dallas Bartley.

Fred Guy, September 11,1952.
Instrument Played: Guitar
Played With: Duke Ellington for 25 years.

Al Hibbler, October 6,1993, December 10,1995.
Occupation: Vocalist
Played With: Dave Jenkins, Clifford Douglas, Jay McShann and Duke Ellington for 8 1/2 years.

Earl Hines, July 21, 1982.
Occupation: Pianist and Bandleader
Instrument Played: Piano
Played With: Louis Armstrong, the Duke Ellington Orchestra, Carroll Dickerson, Jimmie Noone and Erskine Tate.

Milton Hinton, February 22, 1983.

Occupation: Instrumentalist and Instructor
Instruments Played: Bass Fiddle and Violin
Played With: Earl Hines, Jabbo Smith, Eddie South, Fate Marable,
Cab Calloway, Count Basie, Louis Armstrong, Bing Crosby, Pearl
Bailey and Zutty Singleton.

Art Hodes, March 17, 1982.
Occupation: Pianist and Bandleader
Instrument Played: Piano
Played With: Louis Armstrong, Eddie Condon, Sidney Bechet, Bix
Beiderbecke, Bud Freeman, Pops Foster, Pee Wee Russell, Wingy
Manone, Gene Krupa, Chippie Hill and Bunk Johnson.

Franz Jackson, January 5, 1982.
Occupation: Arranger, Composer and Bandleader
Instruments Played: Tenor Saxophone and Clarinet
Played With: Roy Eldridge, Fats Waller, Cootie Williams, Fletcher
Henderson, Earl Hines and Jimmie Noone.

Viola Jefferson
Occupation: Vocalist
Played With: Ray Nance, Horace Henderson, Jimmy Johnson and
Larry Steele's "Smart Affairs." Worked as a single in Europe's night
clubs from 1949 to 1954.

Herb Jeffries, October 28,1994.
Occupation: Vocalist
Played With: Duke Ellington, Earl Hines and as a single.

Eddie Johnson
Occupation: Instrumentalist and Bandleader
Instrument Played: Tenor Saxophone
Played With: Johnny Long, Horace Henderson, Moral Young, Cootie
Williams, Louis Jordan and Coleman Hawkins.

Nat Jones, March 20,1983.
Instrument Played: Saxophone
Played With: Duke Ellington in 1943 at the Hurricane, Tony Fambro,
Johnny Long and Red Saunders.

George Kirby, June 11,1982.
    Occupation: Mimic Extraordinaire, Singer, Dancer and Comedian
Featured In: All major television shows, including Johnny Carson
and Ed Sullivan. Starred in nightclubs and theaters in the continental United States.

Ray Nance, May 20,1972.
    Occupation: Instrumentalist, Vocalist, Dancer and Bandleader
Instruments Played: Trumpet and Violin
Played With: Horace Henderson, Earl Hines and Duke Ellington.

Sy Oliver, April 30, 1982.
    Occupation: Instrumentalist, Arranger, Vocalist, Composer and
Bandleader
Instrument Played: Trumpet
Played With: Zack Whyte, Alphonso Trent, Jimmie Lunceford and
Tommy Dorsey.

Zilmer T. Randolph, September 14,1982.
    Occupation: Composer, Arranger and Director
Instruments Played: Trumpet and Piano
Arranged For: Earl Hines, Duke Ellington, Fletcher Henderson,
Blanche Calloway, Woody Herman, Carroll Dickerson and Dave
Peyton. He also arranged and directed the orchestra for Louis
Armstrong with whom he wrote "Old Man Mose" in 1938. It was
Armstrong's best selling recording until "Hello Dolly."

Herman Roberts, April 8, 1982.
    Occupation: Night Club Owner

William Samuels, June, 1983.
    Occupation: Secretary of Local 208 of the American Federation of
Musicians.

Lonnie Simmons, July 4 and 14, 1983.
    Occupation: Bandleader
Instruments Played: Tenor Saxophone, Clarinet and Organ

Played With: Fats Waller, Hot Lips Page, Savoy Sultons and Ella
Fitzgerald.

Maxine Sullivan
Occupation: Vocalist
Played With: John Kirby, Louis Armstrong, Benny Goodman, Glenn
Gray, Henry Busse, Bobby Hackett and Fats Waller.

Clark Terry, April 4, 1983, December 27 and 29, 1995.
Occupation: Instrumentalist, Composer, Vocalist, Bandleader and
Master Teacher
Instruments Played: Trumpet and Flugle Horn
Played With: Fate Marable, George Hudson, Charlie Ventura, Charlie
Barnet, Eddie "Clean Head" Vinson, Count Basie, Duke Ellington
and the NBC Staff Band for the Johnny Carson's Tonight Show.

Joe Williams, August 26, 1982.
Occupation: Vocalist
Played With: Jimmy Noone, Coleman Hawkins, Lionel Hampton,
Count Basie, Red Saunders, Tiny Parham and Johnny Long.

Nancy Wilson, June, 1983.
Occupation: Vocalist and Actress
Played With: Cannonball Adderley and Larry Steel's "Smart Affairs"
and others.

Dave Young, June 12, 1982.
Instruments Played: Tenor Saxophone and Clarinet
Played With: Roy Eldridge, Carroll Dickerson, Fletcher Henderson,
Horace Henderson, Lucky Millinder, Walter Fuller and King Kolax.

John Young, May 12, 1982.
Occupation: Arranger and Bandleader
Instrument Played: Piano
Played With: Andy Kirk's Orchestra, Joe Williams, Nancy Wilson,
Dick Gregory, Lurlene Hunter and Redd Foxx.

NOTES

The author's diaries and scrapbooks covering his observation and conversations with Mr. Ellington between June, 1936, and 1952.

BOOKS

Anderson, Jervis. This Was Harlem. New York: Farrar Straus Elroux, 1982.

Bigard, Barney. With Louis and the Duke: The Autobiography of a Jazz Clarinetist, ed. Barry Martyn. New York: Oxford University Press; London: Macmillan, 1985.

Calloway, Cab and Bryant Rollins. Of Minnie the Moocher and Me. New York: Thos Y. Crowell Co, 1976.

Chilton, John. Who's Who of Jazz. New York: Time-Life Records Spec Ed, 1978.

Collier, James Lincoln. Duke Ellington. New York: Oxford University Press, 1987.

Cripps, Thomas. Slow Fade to Black. New York: Oxford University Press, 1977.

Dance, Stanley. The World of Duke Ellington. New York: Charles Scribner's Sons, 1970; London: MacMillan, 1971.

Dance, Stanley. The World of Earl Hines. New York: Charles Scribner's Sons, 1977.

Driggs, Frank & Harris Lewine. Black Beauty, White Heat: A Pictorial History of Classical Jazz. New York: Wm Morrow, 1982.

Dubin, Arthur D. Some Classic Trains. Milwaukee: A Kalmback Publication, 1964.

Ellington, Duke. Music is My Mistress. New York: Doubleday & Company, Inc., 1973.

Ellington, Mercer & Stanley Dance. Duke Ellington In Persons: An Intimate Memoir. New York: Da Capo Press, 1978.

Feathers, Leonard. The Encyclopedia of Jazz. New York: Da Capo Press, 1960.

Floyd, Jr., Samuel A. The Power of Black Music. New York: Oxford University Press, 1995.

Gabbard, Krim (editor). Representing Jazz. Duke University Press, 1995.

George, Don. Sweet Man: The Real Duke Ellington. New York: G.P. Putnam's Sons, 1981.

Gleason, Ralph J. Celebrating the Duke, An Atlantic Monthly Press Book. Little Brown and Company, Boston, Toronto 1975.

Hare, Maud Cuney. Negro Musicians and Their Music. New York: Da Capo Press, 1974.

Hasse, John Edward. Beyond Category. New York: Simon & Schuster, 1993.

Hinton, Milton & David G. Berger. Bass Line. Philadelphia: Temple University Press, 1988.

Jewell, Eric. Duke: A Portrait of Duke Ellington. New York: W. W. Norton, 1977.

Jones, LeRoi. Blues People. NY: Wm Morrow, 1963.

Jones, William. The Housing of Negroes in Washington D.C. Washington D.C Howard University Press, 1929.

Ruff, Willie. A Call To Assembly. New York: Penquin Books, 1991.

Shapiro, Nat & Nat Hentoff. The Music Makers. New York: Da Capo Press, 1957.

Stewart, Rex. Boy Meets Horn. ed. Claire P. Gordon. Ann Arbor: University of Michigan Press, 1991.

Stewart, Rex. Jazz Masters of the 30's. New York: Da Capo Press, Inc., 1972.

Travis, Dempsey J. An Autobiography of Black Chicago. Chicago: Urban Research Press, Inc., 1981.

Travis, Dempsey J. An Autobiography of Black Jazz. Chicago: Urban Research Press, 1983.

Tucker, Mark (editor). The Duke Ellington Reader. NY: Oxford University Press, 1993.

MAGAZINES

"Introducing Duke Ellington," Fortune, August, 1933.

"Henderson Will Jam for the Rhythm Cats Mar. 8th," Down Beat, March 1936.

"Goodman Orchestra Plays Next Rhythm Concert Apr. 12," Down Beat, April 1936.

"MCA Takes Over Bands From CBS for $1,000,000," Down Beat, April 1936.

"2nd Rhythm Concert Delights Local "Cats" & "Dogs"," Down Beat, April 1936.

"Goodman & Lombardo Lead Hot & Sweet Bands," Down Beat, May 1936.

"Rhythm Club May Get "Duke" & Spirits Of Rhythm," Down Beat, May 1936.

"Swing Music Will Continue at the Congress Hotel-Ellington Booked," Down Beat, May 1936.

"Duke's Birthday Marks 10th Year of Fame," Down Beat, May 1937.

"Billy Strayhorn-The Young Duke," Jazz, November 5,1943.

"Ellington-Genius of Jazz," Jazz, November 5,1943.

"Critics Tear Hair Over "Dukes" New Tunes-Simplicity Upsets Them,"

Down Beat, March, 1936.

"Duke Says Swing is Stagnant!," Down Beat, February 1939.

"'Situation Between Critics and Musicians is Laughable'-Ellington," Down Beat, April 1939.

"French J-Bugs In Wild Welcome For Ellington," Down Beat, May 1939.

"20 Years of Ellington," Jazz, January 1943.

"Profile: The Hot Bach II," New Yorker, July 1,1944.

"'Beat' Will Again Sponsor Ellington Chicago Concert," Down Beat, February 5, 1950.

"Ellington's Annual Chicago Concert 'A Gala Evening'," Down Beat, March 10,1950.

"He's Too Light Too Be Negro And Too Known To Be White," Ebony 1950.

"Jeffries Sings 'Vital Tones' To Give Women 'Sexual Thrill,'" Ebony 1950.

"Ten Most Promising Crooners," Ebony 1950.

"Mighty Man Of Music," Negro Digest, December 1950.

"Duke Readies New Works For Met Opera House Bow," Down Beat, January 26,1951.

"'Beat' Again To Sponsor Duke's Chicago Concert," Down Beat, February 9,1951.

"Duke's Concert 'Best In Years'," Down Beat, February 23,1951.

"Wined Chicken," Ebony, March 1951.

"Duke Flays NAACP For Halting Richmond Concert," Down Beat, March 9, 1951.

"AFM Cancels Ellington Frisco Concert Onstage," Down Beat, March 23, 1951.

"Duke Hires Tizol, Louie Bellson, Smith," Down Beat, April 20,1951.

"Duke To Do Huge Benefit," Down Beat, May 4,1951.

"Ellington Crew 'Powerful, Thrilling'," Down Beat, May 18,1951.

"Duke's Birdland Success Brings Fast Return Date," Down Beat, June 15, 1951.

"Flock Of Top Musicians Set For Duke's 'DJ' Opus," Down Beat, June 15, 1951.

"Ellington Draws 9,000 To Concert," Down Beat, July 27,1951.

"New Men Continue To Inspire Ellington Band," Down Beat, July 27,1951.

"Duke To End Dearth of Big Jazz Orks In Chicago," Down Beat, August 10, 1951.

"Ellington, Sarah, Nat Packaged For Tour," Down Beat, September 7,1951.

"Barnet Took Basie's Beat, Duke's Harmonics," Down Beat, September 21, 1951.

"Armstrong Scores Triumph In Honolulu Concert Dates," Down Beat, April 4,1952.

"Jazz Knows No Racial Lines, Says Louie Bellson," Down Beat, April 4, 1952.

"Things Ain't What They Ought To Be With Ellington's Band," Down Beat, May 21,1952.

"Miller Memories Paralleled By Growing Lunceford Legend," Down Beat, May 21,1952.

"'Beat' Congratulates A Genius - Edward Kennedy Ellington," Down Beat, May 21,1952.

"Duke Tells Of 10 Top Thrills In 25 Years," Down Beat, May 21,1952.

"The Full Ellington Story Up To His Silver Jubilee," Down Beat, May 21, 1952.

"The Duke's Anniversary," Time, November 3,1952.

"'Beat' Congratulates A Genius-Edward Kennedy Ellington," Down Beat, November 5,1952.

"Carney Sole Survivor Of Original Ellingtonians," Down Beat, November 5,1952.

"Duke Excites, Mystifies Without Any Pretention," Down Beat, November 5,1952.

"Ellington Recalls European Tour, Carnegie, Met Concerts and Other Career Highlights," Down Beat, November 5,1952.

"I Split With Duke When Music Began Sidetracking," Down Beat, November 5,1952.

"Memorial Cottage Planned At Scene Of Blanton's Death," Down Beat, November 5,1952.

"Morton Gould's Tour Of Ellingtonia," Down Beat, November 5,1952.

"Premature Ellington Fan Pays A Mature Tribute," Down Beat, November 5,1952.

"Reminiscing In Tempo-Ned On Early Ellingtonia," Down Beat, November 5,1952.

"Stars, Sidemen and Scribes Offer Tributes To Ellington," Down Beat, November 5,1952.

"The Duke Ellington Story," Down Beat, November 5,1952.

"The Duke's Men, Past And Present," Down Beat, November 5,1952.

"The Ellington Effect," Down Beat, November 5,1952.

"The Full Ellington Story Up To His Silver Jubilee," Down Beat, November 5,1952.

"The Odd Adventures of Ellington Disc Collectors," Down Beat, November 5,1952.

"The Most Exciting Women I've Known," Ebony, May 1953.

"Duke Ellington Employs a 'Stray Horn' Not As Instrument—As An Arranger," New York Age, August 21,1954.

"Swee'pea...," Down Beat, May 30,1956.

"Mood Indigo & Beyond," Time, August 20,1956.

"Duke Ellington," Down Beat(3rd annual yearbook), 1958.

"A Blind Man Can Get Rich," Sepia, December 1958.

"Today's Entertainers Are Thinking, Religious People," Ebony, April 1959.

"Anatomy Of A Murder," Ebony, September, 1959.

"Four Ellingtonians Arrested in Vegas," Down Beat, March 16,1961.

"The 'Jazz Fakers' Can't Make It Now," Negro Digest, November 1961.

"Selection Of Goodman Fires Shot Heard aroung Jazz World," Jet, April 12, 1962.

"Ellington & Strayhorn, Inc.," Down Beat, June 7, 1962.

"Jazz at the Crossroads," Negro Digest, May 1963.

"Ellington The Man," Jazz Beat, February 1964.

"The Ellington Magic," Jazz Beat, January 1966.

"Jazz Goes To Church," Ebony, April, 1966.

"Duke Sets Up Billy Strayhorn Scholarship Fund In New York," Jet, June 22, 1967.

"Duke Ellington," Ebony, July, 1967.

"Eulogy For Sweet Pea," Down Beat, July 13,1967.

"A Medal For Duke and a Kiss For The Chief," Time, May 9,1969.

"Duke Ellington: Greatest Living Popular Musician," Sepia, November, 1972.

"What Did Duke Ellington Know, And When Did He Know It?," Esquire, November, 1973.

"Duke Introduced Sacred Music Concerts," Jet, June 13,1974.

"Duke's Organization Lives Musically And As Business," Jet, June 13,1974.

"Ellington Sought Privacy When Not Playing Onstage," Jet, June 13,1974.

"Ellington Joins Distinguished Musicians and Sidemen In Death," Jet, June 13,1974.

"The Duke Is Remembered," Jet, June 13,1974.

"Thousands Bid Farewell To Duke," Jet, June 13,1974.

"A Tribute To Duke Ellingon," Ebony, September, 1974.

"Duke: Loving You Madly," Essence, September, 1974.

"Clark Terry Jazz Ed, Mumbles Style," Down Beat, November 18,1976.

"Mercer Ellington Extending A Tradition," Down Beat, June 2,1977.

"Dizzy Gillespie Blowin' With Diz, Via Mumble," Down Beat, April 20,1978.

"Son's Revealing Book Says Duke Ellington," Jet, May 25,1978.

"Remembering Duke Ellington," Crisis, January, 1982.

"Profile: Wynton Marsalis," Down Beat, January, 1982.

"Duke Ellington: The Man and His Music," Crisis, April, 1982.

"The Wynton Marsalis Interview," Down Beat, July, 1984.

"Thesis Jazz Pianorama," Crescendo International, November 1987.

"The orchestral Suites Composed by Duke Ellington," Crescendo International, November 1987.

"Wynton Marsalis," Down Beat, November 1987.

"The Further Suite Life of Duke Ellington," Crescendo International, December 1987.

"Blue Note Memories," Reader, August 18,1989.

"A Star Too Soon," National Review, December 31,1989.

"Wynton Prophet in Standard Time," Down Beat, September 1990.

"In Step With: Wynton Marsalis," Parade Magazine, August 16,1992.

"Wynton Marsalis The Professor of Swing," Life Magazine, August 1993.

"Duke Ellington's Black, Brown and Beige," Black Music Research Journal, Fall 1993.

"Wynton & Branford Marsalis A Common Understanding," Down Beat, February 1994.

"Wynton Marsalis America's Most Powerful Jazz Artist Talks About His Latest Work and Lashes White Critics and Gansta Rap," Ebony, July, 1994.

"My Home is the Road," Down Beat, May 1995.

"With Jazz Legend Wynton Marsalis," N'Digo, April 20-May 3,1995

"The New Jazz Age," New York Times Magazine, June 25,1995.

"Marsalis to Trumpet Music Fundamentals on PBS Series," Billboard, August 12,1995.

NEWSPAPERS

"The Harlem Jazz King Burning Up the Stage with His Red-Hot Rhythms," Chicago Herald and Examiner, 16 February 1931.

"All Colored Jamboree," Chicago Herald and Examiner, 17 February 1931.

"'The King Of Jazz' Opens in Gigantic Show at Regal," Chicago Defender, 21 February 1931.

"Ellington and Band to Uptown," Chicago Defender, 28 February 1931.

"Duke and Band Booked to Heat Savoy March 18," Chicago Defender, 7 March 1931.

"Going Backstage With the Scribe," Chicago Defender, 7 March 1931.

"Ellington Comes Back in Response to Thousands of Requests for More Hot Music," Chicago Herald and Examiner, 12 March 1931.

"Melodies! Hot Tunes! Sizzling Syncopation!," Chicago Evening American, 12 March 1931.

"He's Back with a New Program," Chicago Evening American, 13 March 1931.

"Going Backstage With the Scribe," Chicago Defender, 14 March 1931.

"Duke Opens in Detroit on March 20," Chicago Defender, 21 March 1931.

"That Guy Duke Ought to Run for Alderman," Chicago Defender, 21

March 1931.

"Duke Ellington Leads All Others In Popularity Poll Of Nation's Famous Bands," Chicago Defender, 23 March 1931.

"Going Backstage With the Score," Chicago Defender, 28 March 1931.

"Duke Wanted in England at Ciro Club," Chicago Defender, 4 April 1931.

"Going Backstage With the Scribe," Chicago Defender, 11 April 1931.

"Inside Info-," Chicago Defender, 2 May 1931.

"Duke Asks $10,000 for 2nd Picture," Chicago Defender, 9 May 1931.

"Ellington and Band Back at the Oriental," Chicago Defender, 16 May 1931.

"Duke Ellington," New York Amsterdam News, 9 August 1933.

"'Won't You Come Back?' Is Paris' Plea to Ellington," Chicago Defender, 17 August 1933.

"Duke Ellington's Baggage Too Heavy," Chicago Defender, 19 August 1933.

"Freddi Washington Weds," Chicago Defender, 19 August 1933.

"Duke Thinks Well of His Paris Visit," Chicago Defender, 2 September 1933.

"Duke Ellington's Band in West; Due Here Soon," Chicago Defender, 16 September 1933.

"Blue Notes," Chicago Defender, 23 September 1933.

"Duke Stays Here to Include Date at the Savoy," Chicago Defender, 23 September 1933.

"Same Duke New Tunes Arrive in Chicago," Chicago Defender, 23 September 1933.

"Critics Finds Europe copying Duke's Music," Chicago Defender, 11 October 1933.

"Some Stray Notes," New York Amsterdam News, October 1933.

"Cab Not Duke, Dance Lovers' Favorite," Chicago Defender, 30 December 1933.

"Hollywood Greets 'Der Duke' Ellington," New York Amsterdam News, 10 March 1934.

"Duke Ellington A Born Artist," Chicago Defender, 10 March 1934.

"Renowned Conductor Believes Modern Music Is True Expression Of Our Times," Chicago Defender, 10 March 1934.

"Duke Ellington At Cotton Club," Chicago Defender 14 April 1934.

"Ellington Breaks All Records At Coast House," New York Amsterdam News, 14 April 1934.

"Henderson On Tour In the Middle West," New York Amsterdam News, 14 April 1934.

"Duke Ellington Not Only Star Unable to Buy His Soft Drinks," Chicago Defender, 2 June 1934.

"London Advises Mills to Keep Duke Out for While," Chicago Defender, 16 June 1934.

"Duke Ellington Will Be Hired On His Return," New York Amsterdam

News, 23 June 1934.

"Ellington Will Have Regular Show In End," New York Amsterdam News, 23 June 1934.

"Etta Moten Heading Bill at the Lafayette," New York Amsterdam News, 23 June 1934.

"Lunceford and Band No More With Mills," New York Amsterdam News, 23 June 1934.

"The Duke Will Invade The Sunny Southland," New York Amsterdam News, 21 July 1934.

"Ellington To Play At Canadian Exposition," New York Amsterdam News, 11 August 1934.

"Willie Bryant in Return Date At Apollo Theater," New York Amsterdam News, 11 August 1934.

"Ellington Has Another Offer from Paramount," New York Amsterdam News, 22 September 1934.

"Duke Ellington Features At the Apollo Theater," New York Amsterdam News, 6 October 1934.

"Duke Ellington Scores At the Apollo Theater," New York Amsterdam News, 13 October 1934.

"Two-Band Feature at Harlem Opera House," New York Amsterdam News, 6 October 1934.

"Alberta Hunter Still Going Big In England," New York Amsterdam News, 17 November 1934.

"Abbie Mitchell Will Head The Apollo Bill Next Week," New York Amsterdam News, 1 December 1934.

"Duke Ellington In Return Engagement at the Apollo Theater," New York Amsterdam News, 8 December 1934.

"The Duke Scores Again; New Band Coming To Apollo," New York Amsterdam News, 15 December 1934.

"Ellington Plans For Big World Tour Soon," New York Amsterdam News, 2 March 1935.

"Melody Maker Is Still On Louis Armstrong," New York Amsterdam News, 2 March 1935.

"Duke's Engagements Were Not Cancelled," New York Amsterdam News, 15 June 1935.

"Duke Ellington To Top Apollo Theatre Show," New York Amsterdam News, 5 October 1935.

"Ellington Tops To Collegiates," New York Amsterdam News, 15 January 1936.

"Henderson Orchestra to Play Detroit," Chicago Defender, 16 January 1937.

"Ivy Anderson Honor Guest," Chicago Defender, 16 January 1937.

"Duke Ellington Pauses Here Enroute To N.Y.," Chicago Defender, 6 March 1937.

"Duke's Birthday Marks 10th Year of Fame," Chicago Defender, May

1937.

"Ellington Is Denied Concert In London," New York Amsterdam News, 1 April 1939.

"Akron Theatre Back To Vaude With The Duke," Pittsburgh Courier, 15 July 1939.

"Dayton Awaits Coming of Duke," Pittsburgh Courier, 30 September 1939.

"Duke Ellington Opens Hotel Coronado Stay," Chicago Defender, 28 October 1939.

"Man About Town-Town called Hollywood," Pittsburgh Courier, 11 January 1940.

"Duke Ellington Says Days Down Beat Article Gave Wrong Impression," Pittsburgh Courier, 8 February 1940.

"Duke's Band Sensational At Regal," Chicago Defender, 10 February 1940.

"Duke's Band Triumphs At 2 Theaters," Chicago Defender, 17 February 1940.

"Duke's Band Cuts Slides For 2 Days," Chicago Defender, 9 March 1940.

"ASCAP Pays Tribute To Its Members, Lauds Race Composers In Same Breath," Pittsburgh Courier, 10 August 1940.

"Duke Hits 7,000 In Atlanta," Pittsburgh Courier, 24 August 1940.

"Duke Lauded As Greatest," Pittsburgh Courier, 7 September 1940.

"Billy Strayhorn, Jazz Composer and Ellington's Arranger, Dead," New York Times, 1 June 1967.

"Blues Strains Bid Strayhorn Adieu," New York Times, 6 June 1967.

"Duke Ellington Dies, Ends An Era of Great Jazz," Chicago Tribune, 25 May 1974.

"Ellington Rites Jam Cathedral," Chicago Tribune, 25 May 1974.

"Ellington Discography: Treasures Among Duke's Records," Chicago Sun-Times, 2 June 1974.

"Diminuendo, Crescendo in a '74 Musical Score," Chicago Tribune, 5 January 1975.

"Duke Ellington's Son Sells His Pop," Chicago Sun-Times, 28 February 1977.

"In Less Than 3 Minutes, Why Duke Ellington is the Master Arranger," Chicago Tribune, May 13,1984.

"Ellington's 'Pie' Is Ready To Cook," Chicago Tribune, 18 September 1986.

"The Hills and Halls are Alive with Jazz," New York Times, 24 June 1988.

"With Hampton and Marsalis, the 40's and Today," New York Times, 2 July 1988.

"What Jazz Is - and Isn't," New York Times, 31 July 1988.

"Classical Jazz By Modern Masters at Lincoln Center," New York Times, 5 August 1988.

"Tracing the Evolution of Ellington's Art," New York Times, 29 April 1989.

"In Search of the Real Ellington Sound," Wall Street Journal, 8 August 1989.

"Marsalis: The Jazz Missionary," Chicago Tribune, 29 December 1991.

"A Club Date Lets Marsalis Add Flame To His Fame," New York Times, 2 December 1993.

"Wynton Marsalis Takes a Long Look at Slavery," New York Times, 4 April 1994.

"Marsalis Takes Jazz to Church," Chicago Tribune, 2 June 1994.

"Battle of the Titans, With Trumpets," New York Times, 30 June 1994.

"Tooting Terry's Horn," Chicago Tribune, 11 December 1994.

"Marsalis Pulls No Punches in Book," Chicago Tribune, 15 December 1994.

"Keepers of the Flame, and Hot," New York Times, 12 March 1995.

"A Loyalty Test From 'We Know What's Jazz' Crowd," Chicago Tribune, 19 March 1995.

"A Young Pianist Tries to Reinvent the Past," New York Times, 14 May 1995.

"Take The Stray Train," Pittsburgh Post-Gazette, 21 May 1995.

"Marsalis and Friends Play Ellington," New York Times, 18 October 1995.

"Lincoln Center Elevates Status of Jazz," New York Times, 19 December 1995.

"Tale of 2 Trumpeters," Chicago Tribune, 31 December 1995.

"Mercer Ellington, 76, Leader of Father's Band, died Thursday, February 8 in Denmark," New York Times, 10 February 1996.

Ellington on Television

Duke Ellington In Mexico. 1 1/2 hours. 1968.
Love You Madly. 1 hour. 1968.
All I Need Is Love. 1 hour. June 5,1980.
Duke Ellington: The Music Lives On. 1 1/2 hours. August, 1982.
Duke Ellington: The Man. July, 1988.
The American Experience. 1 1/2 hours. November 21,1991.
Reminiscing In Tempo. 1 1/2 hours. April 3,1993.

INDEX